minute foc
Brief Counseling
Techniques that Wo.

MW00987626

TRAUMA
AND ADVERSE
CHILDHOOD EXPERIENCES

Funding to help underwrite the development of
the *15-Minute Focus* series has been generously provided by:

Maclellan Family Foundations

We partner with the courageous
to change the world.

SARAH T. BUTLER
CHILDREN'S CENTER
COLUMBUS, GEORGIA

The Sarah T. Butler Children's Center at the Pastoral Institute of Columbus, Georgia is dedicated to the mental health and well-being of children ages 1-18. This center provides comprehensive services that span psychological testing, intervention, therapy groups, and counseling. In all our activities we seek to inspire growth through faith, hope, and love.

Duplication and Copyright

NATIONAL CENTER for
YOUTH ISSUES
P.O. Box 22185
Chattanooga, TN 37422-2185
423.899.5714 • 866.318.6294
fax: 423.899.4547 • www.ncyi.org

ISBN: 9781937870744
E-book ISBN: 9781953945303
Library of Congress Control Number: 2020913591
© 2020 National Center for Youth Issues, Chattanooga, TN
All rights reserved.
Written by: Dr. Melissa A. Louvar Reeves
Published by National Center for Youth Issues
Printed in the U.S.A. • August 2023

Third party links are accurate at the time of publication, but may change over time.

Contents

See page 101 for information about Downloadable Resources.

Introduction

Taylor is sitting in algebra class, focused on the equation her teacher has written on the board. Suddenly, she hears the sound of heavy footsteps outside the classroom door. Her body instantly reacts—her heart begins to race, her muscles grow tense then tremble, and one part of her brain feels frozen in thought while the other part of her brain says to run! Taylor's teacher calls on her for the answer, but her mind suddenly goes blank. As Taylor stutters the wrong response, the sound of her teacher's footsteps approaching her desk sends Taylor into defense mode. The lion's roar of the teacher's voice elicits an unconscious reaction as Taylor jumps out of the seat with fists clenched and yells, "Get away!" The teacher then yells back. . . .

***

Taylor is not alone. Thirty-five million school-age youth have been exposed to trauma, including acute traumatic events (single time-limited crises, such as car accidents, death, and natural disaster) or chronic traumatic events (multiple crises or adverse childhood experiences, such as poverty, violence, and child maltreatment).[1] To optimize our effectiveness as educators, we must acknowledge the impact of trauma exposure as a contributing factor to school challenges and better understand how to support students. Many students (and staff) have experiences like Taylor. They suffer in silence. Cognitive, social, and emotional development are interrupted. Trauma interferes with the executive functions required to be successful in the classroom, and it impacts our ability to trust our environment and others. For those with repeated trauma exposure, their life may feel like they are constantly walking on eggshells, waiting for the next trauma trigger to occur and never really knowing or trusting how their body and brain will respond. While this book will focus on students and their families, there are many educators who have trauma histories themselves. I hope the content provided in this book can also help educators who have been personally impacted.

As educators, we see the behaviors, but we don't always consider or understand why these behaviors occur. I began my career as a special education teacher who specialized in working with students with emotional and behavioral challenges. I was trained primarily as a behaviorist. Most behaviors can be explained by analyzing the antecedents, behaviors, and consequences of observable behaviors. Thus, behaviors can then be modified or influenced if there are strong enough reinforcers or punishment. What was missing over twenty years ago in my teacher training program was understanding and identifying trauma. As I reflect back to the students I worked with early in my career, it saddens me to think how many of those students had trauma histories that were never acknowledged, validated, or addressed through trauma-informed practices. No wonder so many only showed temporary gains (they were only responding to the immediate reinforcers) and minimal long-term progress. While strategies using behaviorist theories can be effective, they are insufficient for those with trauma histories. These students need and deserve more from us. What we can do does not require a lot of extra effort; it just requires patience, understanding, and a different approach to addressing behaviors.

In this book, I will identify the different types of stress and the symptoms that accompany trauma exposure. I will highlight the commonalities between externalizing disorders as well as trauma- and stressor-related disorders. Too often, trauma is confused with willful oppositional behaviors. We will also explore the overlap with anxiety. I strongly suggest you read another book in this series by Leigh Bagwell titled *Educator's Guide to Helping Students with Anxiety*. Leigh's book further describes anxiety that can underlie trauma exposure and provides great resources for anxiety management. I will provide practical strategies for school mental health professionals (school counselors, school psychologists, school social workers, and school nurses), along with strategies for administrators, teachers, and parents. It is also important to realize that some types of trauma exposure may require intensive services beyond what a school can provide. Thus, we will review effective school and research-based psychotherapeutic treatments. Lastly, I will provide additional resources to further your understanding of trauma identification and multitiered, trauma-informed interventions.

Most importantly, trauma is treatable!

Through trauma informed practices, educators and school mental health professionals can make positive impacts on the lives of those affected by trauma. As former president of the National Association of School Psychologists, my presidential theme was "Small Steps Change Lives." I hope this book will help you take the small steps needed to make a big difference in changing the lives of students, teachers, and parents. Increased understanding regarding trauma and effective interventions helps us to provide better supports that facilitate growth and achievement in all areas of life. We may truly be the lifeline that provides the hope and encouragement an individual needs to integrate the trauma experience into who they are, without letting it completely define what they become.

1 What Is Trauma?

The term "ACEs," or Adverse Childhood Experiences, has received increased attention in education over the past decade. ACEs are defined as potentially traumatic events that occur in childhood (zero to seventeen years) to include the following: experiencing violence, abuse, or neglect; witnessing violence in the home or community; having a family member attempt suicide or die by suicide; being raised in an environment that undermines a sense of safety and stability; and exposure to traumatic events that impact a person's ability to emotionally attach to others such as substance misuse/abuse, mental health problems, and/or instability due to parental separation or family members being incarcerated.

A hallmark study initiated in 1994 by Kaiser Permanente and the Center for Disease Control measured a variety of ACEs and their relationship to health and social problems.[2] What they discovered is ACEs are common and highly interrelated. Almost two-thirds of study participants reported at least one ACE, and nearly one in six reported they had experienced four or more types of ACEs. Women and several racial/ethnic minority groups were at higher risk for having experienced four or more types of ACEs, and some children were at greater risk than others.

This study also discovered how ACEs impact all aspects of a person's life. The graphic below summarizes the cumulative negative effects of ongoing toxic stress and trauma exposure.

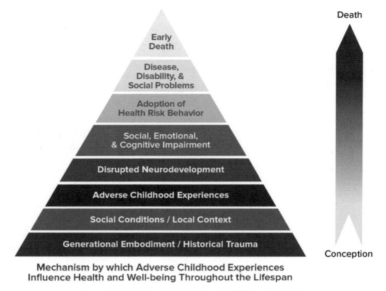

Death

Early
Death

Disease,
Disability, &
Social Problems

Adoption of
Health Risk Behavior

Social, Emotional,
& Cognitive Impairment

Disrupted Neurodevelopment

Adverse Childhood Experiences

Social Conditions / Local Context

Generational Embodiment / Historical Trauma

Conception

**Mechanism by which Adverse Childhood Experiences
Influence Health and Well-being Throughout the Lifespan**

Sources: Center for Disease Control and Prevention (2020). In public domain.[3]

Current research supports a strong, predictive correlation
between ACEs and negative outcomes. ACEs have a "dose-
response" reaction, meaning as the number of adverse childhood
experiences increases, the risk of developing significant health
and mental problems gradually accumulates. For children,
growing up in an environment with toxic stress can lead to
difficulty forming healthy and stable relationships. This then leads
to unstable work histories as adults, which can then lead to
depression and limited educational and economic opportunities.
The effects of the toxic stress can then be passed onto their own
children (generational trauma). Toxic stress is often compounded
by the historical and ongoing traumas due to systemic racism and
poverty, which leads to living in under-resourced and/or racially
segregated neighborhoods. These living conditions often lead
to food insecurity and forced frequent moves. The cumulative
effects of the toxic stress then lead to chronic health problems,
substance misuse/abuse, and mental illness, including suicide.
And to further compound development, ACEs also negatively
impact brain development, academic achievement, and the
ability to develop social-emotional competencies and executive

functions such as attention, decision-making, learning, and responding to stress— the exact skills needed for academic and occupational success. In summary, the academic, emotional, social, and economic costs to families, communities, and society is great. Are you feeling defeated yet?

On so many levels ACEs can seem impossible to overcome. However, trauma is treatable and ACEs are preventable! By acknowledging the impact of trauma and implementing trauma informed practices, we can create and sustain safe, stable, nurturing relationships and environments for all children and families. We can help to prevent and/or mitigate the negative impact of ACEs and help all children reach their full potential. Our small steps can change lives!

Science shows the effects of ACEs are not permanent.[4]

Stress vs. Crisis vs. Trauma

Humans experience different types of stress and trauma exposures, yet these experiences are highly interrelated as they determine how we cope and respond.

Stress

Stress can actually be a good thing! *Yeah right*, you may be thinking. *How can stress be good when we are more stressed now than we have ever been?* But it's true. At the same time, however, stress can also be toxic. Thus, it's important to distinguish among three kinds of stress responses: positive, tolerable, and toxic.

Positive Stress   Tolerable/Acute Stress   Toxic Stress   Post-Traumatic Stress

Positive stress helps us take action when we are uncomfortable and is essential for normal development. It is characterized by brief increases in heart rate and mild elevations in hormone levels. For example, positive stress might occur when a child begins their first day of school or is receiving an immunization shot. It may also be initiated by an impending deadline that motivates us to get the project done. Stress is experienced when you find yourself in an unsafe situation and your brain and body are told to take action to get to a safer location. Positive stress is a moderate, short-lived stress response, and when the stressor subsides, the body returns to a calm baseline.

Tolerable (acute) stress is potentially harmful, but relatively short-lived. For example, an acute stressor is the loss of a loved one, a natural disaster, or a frightening injury that activates the body's alert systems for a longer period of time than positive stress. It requires the use of coping strategies and can be buffered by supportive adult relationships that help the child to adapt, thus mitigating the potential damaging effects on the brain and body. The child learns to adapt and integrate the experience into their life narrative as they move forward, adjusting to the "new normal." Thus, not all stressful situations are a crisis.

Toxic stress is strong, frequent, prolonged activation of stress mechanisms that often occurs when a child experiences adverse childhood experiences without adequate adult support. When prolonged activation of the stress response systems occurs continuously, or is triggered by multiple stressors, the cumulative effects take a toll on an individual's physical and mental health and disrupt body and brain development. However, research also indicates that supportive, responsive relationships with caring adults, particularly if these relationships are available early in life, can help to prevent or reverse the damaging effects of toxic stress response.

Crisis

A *crisis* is perceived as extremely negative, can generate feelings of helplessness, powerlessness, and/or entrapment, and may occur suddenly, unexpectedly, and without warning. It leads to a temporary state of upset and disorganization that overwhelms an individual's ability to cope and has the potential for positive and/or negative outcomes. Thus, a crisis that is effectively managed can be considered tolerable (acute) stress. However, a crisis not effectively managed, or the continual accumulation of stressors, can lead to toxic stress.

When toxic stress is ongoing and is combined with ongoing chronic trauma, post-traumatic stress can develop. Post-traumatic stress often begins as a normal response to stress and trauma, but the reactions become prolonged and begin to impact physical and emotional health.

Thus, does exposure to a crisis mean an individual will develop toxic stress or post-traumatic stress? No. While this may be the case for some, this is not the case for all. While crisis exposure and trauma are correlational, the relationship is not necessarily causal. Resiliency and supports can mitigate the negative impacts of trauma exposure and help an individual adjust.

A crisis is the event, experience, or condition that leads to danger or the potential for danger.

Trauma is the result of an individual's reaction to the crisis event.

Acute vs. Chronic/Complex Trauma

Trauma reactions are the result of actual or perceived harm to one's physical, psychological, or emotional well-being. What makes the crisis experience traumatic is the individual's reaction, not just the experience itself. Cultural context also matters. For example, in cultures where women are viewed as inferior or keeping the family together avoids public shame, domestic violence may be seen as more tolerable and disclosure and expression of traumatic stress may not occur. These individuals may not perceive this as trauma and/or will suffer in silence for fear of the consequences of disclosure, but their body and mind still feel the impact.

There is also a distinction regarding the different types of trauma experiences—acute versus chronic trauma. **Acute trauma** exposure is of time-limited duration (car accidents, natural disasters, loss of a family member, etc.). When a threatening acute stressor is perceived (i.e. scary dog), the body releases stress hormones (adrenaline and cortisol) that increase heart rate and blood pressure and prepare the body to either flight, fight, or freeze. When the threat is gone, the body returns to baseline. The brain becomes calm again and is available for learning and prosocial interactions. Supportive adults and social-emotional lessons (e.g. anxiety management) can help students learn how to do this.

Acute Trauma:

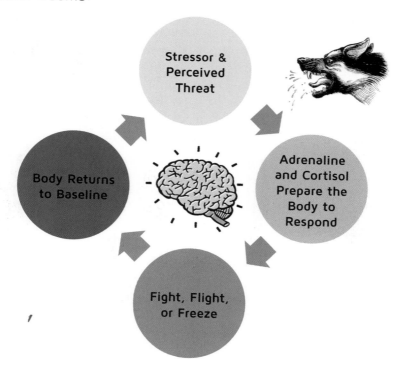

Stressor & Perceived Threat

Adrenaline and Cortisol Prepare the Body to Respond

Fight, Flight, or Freeze

Body Returns to Baseline

Chronic/complex trauma is continual and ongoing exposure to toxic stress that continues or repeats for months or years at a time. It usually begins early in life, disrupts development including the formation of a self, and interferes with the child's ability to form a secure attachment bond with caregivers (we will talk about this more in chapter 4.).

When the threatening stressor (i.e. scary dog) is perceived by an individual with a history of ongoing trauma exposure, the body responds; however, there is no complete return to baseline. The body and brain feels like it is living on pins and needles most of the time. A person can't experience safety when the scary dog is constantly living in their brain (and maybe also in their house or neighborhood). The scary dog is always lurking around the corner or they "see the dog" everywhere, scared an attack could occur at any time. The brain is constantly interrupted which makes learning difficult, and emotional regulation and relationships are negatively impacted.

Complex/Chronic Trauma

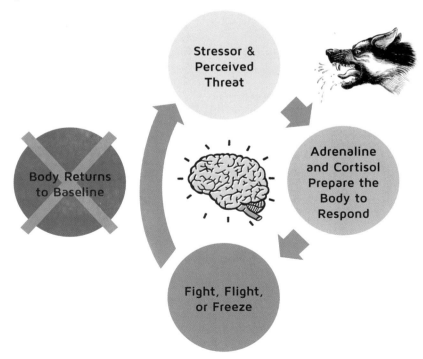

For some, traumatic stress reactions may last several weeks or months but generally start to subside if a child experiences no other traumas and has resiliency and supports in place to help cope with the stress. For example, a child who witnessed her parent being killed as a result of domestic violence may initially be preoccupied with her own safety and criminal justice processes. Once she is reassured that she is safe and will be protected, and she has effective supports in place, she may not show further signs of traumatic stress. She may, however, begin to express her grief about the loss of her parent. Her traumatic stress reactions do not develop into toxic stress or post-traumatic stress. However, take this same situation with a child who does not have resiliency or supports, and there are ongoing secondary stressors such as the loss of a home, needing to relocate to live with relatives, changing schools, and losing peer support. This child is more likely to exhibit toxic or post-traumatic stress reactions.

Trauma Triggers

For those with a trauma history, there are often trauma triggers that activate the trauma reactions described above. Common triggers include:

- loud, chaotic environments
- threatening gestures
- certain odors (specifically those related to the trauma experience)
- physical touch
- sounds (fire alarm, sounds of emergency vehicles and emergency personnel, music that is connected to the event or loss)
- confinement or feeling trapped
- unclear/uncertain expectations
- change in routine (especially without notice)

- authority figures that try to set limits through demands (instead of providing choices)
- witnessing an altercation or violence between other individuals
- spaces that remind them of trauma experience (low lighting, bathrooms, unsupervised areas)
- feelings (anger, sadness, or fear) in response to common school conflicts (being approached by another student, getting in trouble, doing poorly on a test, being called stupid or unmotivated)

Impact on Brain Development

"We tend to divide the work of mental health separate from the world of physical health, but the body doesn't do that."
—Dr. Nadine Burke Harris[5]

Trauma can change the brain. There is much research that supports the idea that traumatized brains look different from non-traumatized brains, with three main areas of the brain being significantly impacted. The "thinking center" (prefrontal cortex, or PFC) and "emotion regulation center" (anterior cingulate cortex, or ACC) are underactivated; whereas the "fear center" (amygdala) is overactivated. The thinking center is most impacted by deprivation (neglect) due to lack of stimulation, and the emotional regulation center is most impacted by trauma and violence.

The Whole-Brain Child is a great book that describes the impact of trauma on the brain in a way that students, educators, and parents can understand.[6] They use the analogy that our brains are like a house. The upstairs contains our prefrontal and neocortex, our "thinking brain." Characters such as Calming Charlie, Problem Solving Paul, Creative Carrie, and Flexible Fred are the thinkers, problem solvers, planners, and emotion regulators who are creative, flexible, and empathic toward others. The downstairs is our limbic system (amygdala), our "feeling brain," which is very focused on keeping us safe and making sure our needs are met. This is where the instinct for survival originates. The characters that live downstairs, Alerting Alice, Frightened Freddie, and Big Boss Buddy, help us look out for danger and will sound the alarm when there is a threat and we need to fight, run, or hide.

Our brains work best, and we learn best, when the upstairs and the downstairs work together and can carry messages up and down the stairs to each other. This allows us to make good choices, maintain friendships, come up with exciting and creative games to play, problem solve when in an uncomfortable situation, and calm ourselves down when we are stressed or scared. When one of the characters in the downstairs brain spots some danger, the downstairs brain ("feeling brain") takes over and "flips the lid" on the upstairs brain ("thinking brain"), which exposes our amygdala and emotions take over. The pathway that normally allows the upstairs and downstairs to work together is no longer connected, and our brains become overwhelmed with feelings such as fear, sadness, or anger.

What happens when **YOU FLIP YOUR LID**

PREFRONTAL CORTEX IS ENGAGED:

Calm, rational thought, mental flexibility. Able to make good decisions.

LID IS FLIPPED --> AMYGDALA IS ENGAGED

Big emotions arise—anger, fear, anxiety, sadness. Unable to make good decisions or calm down.

Source: The Whole Brain Child

The upstairs brain (neocortex or "thinking brain") can work properly again when we are out of danger. How long does it take to return to equilibrium and resume learning? That depends if exposure is a positive or tolerable/acute stressor or a toxic, chronic stressor. If an individual experiences toxic stress, they are at increased risk for their body not returning to baseline (the downstairs brain stays activated). They experience chronic stress, vigilance, fear, and irritation and also have a hard time feeling safe, calming down, managing emotions, or sleeping; all symptoms of a hyperactive amygdala. In addition, they experience more difficulties with concentration and attention and struggle more to think clearly—all symptoms of the thinking center being underactivated.

A Student's Story

Taylor did not mean to jump out of her seat and yell at her teacher. She actually loves her algebra teacher. But due to being a victim of sexual abuse and hearing the sound of footsteps just before her uncle enters her room late at night to abuse her (trauma trigger), she "flipped her lid" and her emotional and physical responses took over. Due to the ongoing abuse, even when she wants to calm down and feel better, she can't. There are just too many reminders, too many trauma triggers. Teachers and peers perceive her as a "loose cannon" who can't control her temper. Now she is headed for her third out-of-school suspension this semester.

Taylor's brain is also experiencing developmental trauma. Survival is her brain's focus, with little energy left for social/emotional regulation and cognitive processing. Whereas the brain of a non-traumatized student can focus on cognition (learning) and social/emotional regulation, with little energy needed for survival and regulation.

Trauma & Brain Development

Acute Trauma

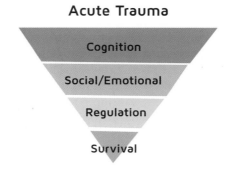

Cognition

Social/Emotional

Regulation

Survival

Developmental/Chronic Trauma

Cognition

Social/Emotional

Regulation

Survival

Adapted from Holt & Jordan, Ohio Dept. of Education

Source: https://sharedparentinginfo.com/563/

Taylor is not trying to be the "bad kid." She just needs someone to understand. She needs someone to help her learn how to identify her trauma triggers so she can implement emotional regulation and anxiety management strategies. Her amazing teacher could benefit from staff development to better understand trauma.

QUESTIONS
to
CONSIDER

1. What is Taylor's trauma history?

2. What are her trauma triggers?

3. What parts of her brain are under- and overactivated?

4. How have her academics and relationships been impacted by trauma?

5. What resources are available to Taylor, her teachers, and her parents?

KEY POINTS

- There are different types of stress and trauma exposure. Not all are bad. Resiliency and social supports make a difference in outcomes.
- Trauma impacts brain development. Behavior is not always a conscious choice but a trauma response to a perceived threat.
- Trauma is treatable!

2

What Does Trauma Look Like?

The signs and symptoms of trauma are easy to miss. The internalized symptoms are hard to detect, and the externalizing symptoms are often mistaken for behavioral disorders. Many students (and adults) with trauma histories suffer in silence. They are often too afraid or ashamed to share their experience or too scared they will be seen as "crazy." For those students living in chronic abuse or neglect situations, they are afraid that revealing the abuse could result in removal from the home, their only caregiver being arrested, and/or the primary breadwinner being removed, thus leading to financial hardships. As one of my former students once said to me, "Having a home is better than no home."

Trauma exposure can affect any of the following:

Academics/Cognitive	Behavioral	Social and Personal
• organization • comprehension • memory • ability to produce work • engagement in learning • classroom tasks and instructions • grasping of cause-and-effect relationships • language development • meeting academic standards	• self-regulation • attention • emotions—act out or withdraw, depression, anxiety • behavior • attendance • substance abuse	• development of language and communication skills • difficulties processing social skills • establishment of a coherent sense of self • trust • emotional regulation • self-harm • anxiety • depression

From the student's perspective, they don't feel safe. To gain a sense of control, they will "flip" into the trauma world and their survival brain is activated. The rules are different in the trauma world, as emotional and physical survival take priority.

Yet, many students exposed to trauma are misunderstood and described by teachers as:

- naughty
- manipulative
- avoidant
- can't be trusted
- unmotivated
- refuses to listen
- ignores teachers; ignores others
- doesn't do their homework
- misses school for no reason
- a liar
- lazy
- blames others
- overreacts
- doesn't take school seriously
- makes excuses
- doesn't care about school

When adults describe a student in negative terms, the student begins to internalize this negativity and it makes functioning in school difficult. Their thought process now becomes:

- I'm worthless/nothing.
- I can't trust anybody.
- There is no point in asking for help.
- I will always be abandoned.
- I will be punished if I speak up.
- There is danger everywhere.
- Feelings are dangerous.
- I'm a bad kid and there is nothing I can do to change my life.
- Nobody notices when I try anyway so why keep trying.
- They won't believe me that I am trying to change.

Their trauma reactions are often misinterpreted as defiant, uncooperative, or unmotivated behaviors, thus many end up suspended or expelled, further disconnecting them from supports and resources. As counselors and school mental health professionals, we can help educate our colleagues on the signs and symptoms of trauma so the behaviors of students are more accurately understood. In addition, we can help teachers implement strategies that avoid power struggles and conflict. We can be the broker between the trauma and educational worlds.

Psychological Triage

So how do we identify traumatic impact? This can be done by conducting psychological triage. Triage means to identify, sort, and prioritize. This helps to ensure appropriate supports are provided based upon demonstrated need, as there are consequences to over- or under-responding. Primary triage occurs as soon as the crisis takes place but before supports are provided. It is the initial identification and sorting of who will get the most directive supports first. Secondary triage takes place as initial interventions are delivered. Reactions are monitored for common or atypical/extreme reactions. This directs next steps for supports. Referral (tertiary) triage typically takes place after common reactions have been given time to subside, the school crisis interventions conclude, and/or the individual becomes so emotionally overwhelmed that supports outside of the school are needed immediately (for example, in a suicide attempt).

Primary Triage	Secondary Triage	Referral Triage
Establishes initial treatment priorities	Uses data collected during interventions	Is conducted as interventions conclude

Source: Brock & Reeves[8]

For accurate initial identification through psychological triage, we must consider the crisis event characteristics and variables.

Crisis Characteristics

The crisis characteristics include an individual's perception of the event, one's sense of control, and if the event was sudden or unexpected. If the individual perceives the event as scary, they didn't know what do to and they had no forewarning to prepare, the higher the potential traumatic impact.

Crisis Event Variables (the "event type")

Predictability, Duration, Consequences, Intensity

Crisis event characteristics interact with crisis event variables. Traumatic events that are *unpredictable*, last longer (*duration*), involve interpersonal assaultive violence (*intensity*), and result in the death of a close friend or loved one (*consequences*) have greater levels of traumatic impact. While those events that are *predictable* (loss of a primary caregiver due to a long-term illness) can still be traumatic, they tend to have lower levels of traumatic impact due to having time to prepare for the loss.

Crisis events that are longer in *duration* can increase the feeling of uncontrollability. This is why we practice crisis drills in schools. While we may not be able to stop the crisis event from occurring, knowing what to do to get to a safe place provides a sense of control which can lessen traumatic impact. In addition, the longer the traumatic stressor creates coping challenges, the higher the risk for developing anxiety, despair, and depression.

The *intensity* of the personal crisis experience is influenced by proximity. Greater PTSD symptoms are seen in individuals with closer *physical proximity* to the actual event and greater sensorial experiences (victim or direct witness to violence; high intensity sounds and visual images) as these experiences leave a greater traumatic imprint of memories on the brain. *Emotional proximity*, the emotional attachment/relationship to the victim, also contributes greatly to traumatic reactions.

The crisis characteristics and event type variables then interact with personal internal and external vulnerabilities to determine the individual's threat perception.

Vulnerabilities (the "experience")

Threat perception is an individual subjective appraisal of the event. The scarier or more traumatizing an individual perceives the event, the higher the correlation with development of traumatic reactions. Research has shown a person's subjective appraisal is more important than the objective threat. If adults stay calm, students/children perceive the event as less scary. Thus, parent and teacher reactions play a significant role in threat perceptions, particularly for younger children. If a parent/ teacher copes well, the student/child is more likely to cope well. If the parent/teacher is struggling, there is increased likelihood the child will struggle. The analogy here is if a child falls off a swing and the parent rushes over in a panic, the child will start to cry. If the parent stays calm, gives the child a "boo-boo kiss," picks them back up, smiles, and encourages them to get back on the swing, the child is more than likely to do so and not be as scared.

We cannot ignore how media and social media significantly influence threat perceptions. The exposure to everyday negative, non-stop news can be frightening and escalate threat perceptions, particularly for young children who may not understand or realize the event is far away or rare. Socially anxious children also display lower thresholds for threat perceptions, and increased depression is associated with threat perception distortions. Research supports that increased social media and television use is associated with elevated perceptions of personal vulnerability to world threats, greater anxiety, and also influences copycat events and contagion.

Vulnerabilities

Vulnerabilities are the flip side of resiliency and increase risk for traumatic impact. Students with *internal vulnerabilities* include those with preexisting mental illness, neurobiological vulnerabilities due to toxic stress/ACEs, difficulties regulating emotions, and decreased self-esteem. However, SEL (social emotional learning) instruction can help to build their "tool kit" with strategies to mitigate risk factors even before crisis exposure ever occurs. (Read more about this in chapters 5–7.)

Typically, low cognitive ability (as evident by those receiving special education services for an intellectual disability) is an internal vulnerability. While these students are at higher risk for increased traumatic impact due to not having the abilities to cognitively understand and process the event, their low cognitive ability level could also serve as a protective factor if they do not perceive the event as scary. If this is the case, we do not want to tell them details or respond in a way that will increase their fears, as this could unnecessarily escalate threat perceptions. Conducting psychological triage and paying attention to one's threat perception is critical to ensuring we do not over- or underreact to meet student needs.

External vulnerabilities include absence of family support and resources, poor family functioning, parental traumatic stress and/or mental illness, family history of PTSD, social isolation, low or perceived lack of social support, bias and discrimination, and poverty. These all contribute to the development of trauma reactions. A focus on building external resiliency and social supports for self and family, increasing family connectedness, and engagement in prosocial activities can help build buffers to mitigate external vulnerabilities. Schools are a critical part of this solution as this is what we do! There are many individuals exposed to a traumatic stressor(s) that go on to lead healthy and successful lives because of supports received in school.

The graphic below summarizes the interaction of trauma event variables and the individual's personal experience that helps determine the potential development of traumatic reactions.

The PREP<u>a</u>RE Model of Psychological Triage

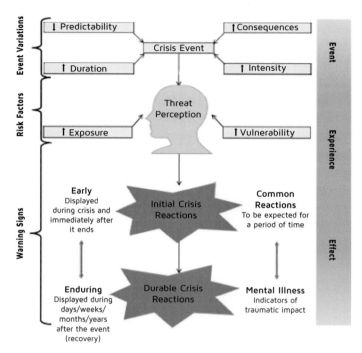

Adapted from: Brock, S. & Reeves, M. (2019). PREP<u>a</u>RE WS2 (3rd Ed): Mental Health Crisis Intervention: Responding to an Acute Traumatic Stressor in Schools. National Association of School Psychologist. Bethesda, MD. Primary author.[9]

Trauma Reactions (the "effect")

For those exposed to an acute traumatic event, some reactions are to be expected for a period of time. The goal for schools is to provide crisis intervention supports to mitigate the traumatic impact so the common crisis reactions described below are temporary.

Common Initial Crisis Reactions

Emotional	Physical
• Shock	• Fatigue
• Anger	• Insomnia
• Despair	• Sleep disturbance
• Emotional numbing	• Hyperarousal/overly alert
• Terror or fear	• Startle response
• Guilt	• Somatic complaints
• Phobias	• Impaired immune response
• Depression	• Headaches
• Sadness	• Gastrointestinal problems
• Grief	• Decreased appetite
• Irritability	• Decreased libido
• Hypersensitivity	• Startle response
• Helplessness	
• Hopelessness	
• Loss of pleasure from activities	
• Dissociation[a]	

Cognitive	Interpersonal/Behavioral
• Impaired concentration	• Alienation
• Impaired decision-making ability	• Social withdrawal or isolation
• Memory impairment	• Increased relationship conflict
• Disbelief	• Vocational impairment
• Confusion	• Refusal to go to school
• Distortion	• Aggression
• Decreased self-esteem	• School impairment
• Decreased self-efficacy	• Avoidance of reminders
• Self-blame	• Crying easily
• Intrusive thoughts or memories[b]	• Change in eating patterns
• Worry	• Tantrums
• Nightmares	• Regression in behavior
	• Risk taking

Source: Brock et al 2019.[10]
a. Examples include perceptual experiences reported as being dreamlike, having tunnel vision, feeling spacey, or being on automatic pilot.
b. Reenactment play among children.

So how long do common reactions manifest themselves? While it is important to realize that individual responses and the path to recovery can vary. According to the U.S. Department of Homeland Security, survivors of traumatic events who do not manifest symptoms after approximately two months generally do not require follow-up.[11]

Developmental Specific Reactions

While the chart above has general common reactions, it is also important to recognize the developmental specific reactions. In general, the crisis reactions of preschool youth are not as clearly connected to the crisis event. Reexperiencing the trauma can be expressed via generalized nightmares, trauma-related play, non-verbal reactions to include tantrums, crying, screaming, clinginess, shaking/trembling, and scared facial expressions. They can also regress back to wetting or soiling their pants, thumb-sucking, fear of the dark, and/or difficulties with parental separation.

For kindergarten through second grade students, the reactions are more directly connected to the event. Behavioral indicators include clinginess or anxious attachment behaviors, behavioral regression, irritability, anxiety, and school refusal. Decreased emotional regulation such as irrational fears, fighting with peers, and outbursts of anger are also seen along with psychosomatic symptoms that include stomachaches and headaches. Thus, it is important to put school nurses on alert.

Third through fifth grade students often reexperience the event through play, but the play is often more elaborate to include drawings, writing, and pretend play. School problems such as difficulties paying attention, poor academic performance, and increased behavioral problems, in addition to repetitive verbal descriptions of the event (without appropriate affect), can also be observed.

Adolescents begin to develop abstract reasoning abilities; thus, their crisis reactions are more similar to adults. However, trauma reactions are often misidentified as oppositional and aggressive behaviors. Difficulties with social relationships and school performance, in addition to self-injurious behaviors, suicidal ideation, school avoidance, revenge fantasies, and self-medication with substances, are often evident in traumatized adolescents.

It is also important for school mental health professionals to consider cultural and religious beliefs. Understanding cultural-specific reactions that communicate pain and suffering, and expressions of grief and loss, help to prevent the over-pathologizing of reactions that are culturally specific. Culture also influences threat perceptions, how individuals assign meaning to a threat and their own personal reactions, and what and whom they view as helpful supports. Thus, if unfamiliar with a student's culture, find someone who is familiar to provide guidance. Culturally sensitive counselors are critical to one's recovery.

Chronic Trauma/ACEs

Without proper supports, common reactions can turn into enduring reactions (PTSD or acute stress disorder). In addition to the reactions above and formal PTSD symptoms (see chapter 3), those exposed to chronic trauma often report the following additional difficulties and symptoms:

Traumatic Impact	Symptoms/Reactions
Emotional Regulation	persistent sadness, suicidal thoughts, explosive anger, or inhibited anger
Consciousness	includes forgetting traumatic events, reliving traumatic events, or having episodes in which one feels detached from one's mental processes or body (dissociation)
Self-Perception	may include helplessness, shame, guilt, stigma, and a sense of being completely different from other human beings; changes in self-concept
Distorted Perceptions of the Perpetrator	attributing total power to the perpetrator, becoming preoccupied with the relationship to the perpetrator, or preoccupied with revenge
Relations with Others	isolation, distrust, or a repeated search for a rescuer
One's System of Meanings	loss of sustaining faith or a sense of hopelessness and despair
Maladaptive Coping	alcohol and substance abuse to avoid and/or numb their feelings and thoughts; self-mutilation, suicidal ideation, and other forms of self-harm

If the reactions above are enduring (they do not lessen with time and/or worsen), they begin to impact sense of self and life functioning. Therapeutic supports and trauma-focused therapies are often needed to help address these reactions (see chapter 8).

Positive Consequences

While most of the attention goes to negative consequences, it is also important to focus on the positive consequences. Short-term positive impacts of trauma exposure include bringing the community together, bringing attention to individual and community needs, and activating resources. Long-term positive impacts include building coping skills, implementing prevention programs (i.e. trauma informed approaches), and increasing monies to enhance physical and psychological safety and to address inequities. Thus, the activation of positive consequences can help to mitigate the negative effects described in this chapter.

A Student's Story

Twelve-year-old Andreas immigrated to the United States three years ago. His parents are currently in jail after being arrested in their home country for participating in the prodemocracy movement. His family witnessed significant community violence and even had death threats on their own lives. He and his younger sibling were sent to America to live with their aunt, uncle, and grandparents (also political refugees). He doesn't know if he will ever see his parents again. While he likes and feels safe at school, he is struggling academically. He had limited formal schooling prior to coming to the US and is still struggling to learn English. His uncle recently lost his job and his maternal grandfather died five weeks ago. He is trying to stay focused in school but is preoccupied with how he can make money to support the family. He is falling further behind academically and rarely speaks anymore in class. He's afraid to tell his teachers what is going on. While his aunt and grandparents are in the country legally, his uncle is not. He's afraid if he talks, his uncle will be deported.

QUESTIONS
to
CONSIDER

1. What type of stress and trauma is Andreas experiencing?

2. What school associated trauma difficulties and trauma reactions are present?

3. What are his internal and external vulnerabilities?

KEY POINTS

1. It is important to interpret behavior through the trauma lens.

2. Trauma exposure can have both positive and negative outcomes.

3. Triage is an ongoing process to help identify, sort, and prioritize who needs help and the appropriate interventions to provide.

4. The effects of trauma exposure are a result of the crisis characteristics and event variables (predictability, duration, consequences, intensity) interacting with the type of experience (exposure, vulnerabilities) to determine one's threat perceptions and reactions.

5. It is important to be culturally informed and understand the difference between common/initial crisis reactions and durable/long-lasting reactions. Do not over-pathologize!

What Are Trauma- and Stressor-Related Disorders?

Trauma- and stressor-related disorders, as defined by the DSM-5, include those disorders for which exposure to a traumatic or stressful event is explicitly listed as a diagnostic criterion. In addition, these disorders also have a timeframe for which the symptoms must be manifested before a diagnosis can be made. This is intentional so common reactions are not misidentified as pathological. Research has shown that an individual with four or more ACEs is thirty-two times more likely to have learning and behavior problems.[12]

While school mental health professionals may not formally diagnose according to the DSM-5, they need to be aware of the diagnostic criterion as they are often the front lines to first identify the signs and symptoms of trauma exposure. School mental health professionals are also critical to ensuring accurate identification as trauma reactions are often misidentified as oppositional behaviors or learning problems.

All behaviors send a message.

In addition, trauma-associated challenges, if severe enough, may qualify a student for additional services through a 504 plan or Individualized Education Plan (IEP-special education). Thus, early identification and intervention are critical to helping a student onto a more positive academic and life course.

Trauma- and stressor-related disorders include: Reactive Attachment Disorder, Disinhibited Social Engagement Disorder, Post-traumatic Stress Disorder (PTSD), Acute Stress Disorder, and

Adjustment Disorder. The latter three will be the focus of this chapter, as these are more commonly seen in schools. For more in-depth information, read the *Diagnostic and Statistical Manual of Mental Disorders, Fifth Edition* (DSM-5).

Before we get into the clinical aspects of trauma, it is important to acknowledge the following:

1. Trauma occurs on a continuum.
2. A student does not have to be diagnosed with PTSD to have symptoms of trauma or complex trauma.
3. Symptoms of trauma are an individual response.
4. Do not judge someone's trauma.
5. What is a trauma for one person may not be for another.
6. It is the symptoms (not the event) that define where they are on the trauma response continuum. Some reactions are normal (common) and to be expected, whereas others may need more formalized mental health treatment.

Post-Traumatic Stress Disorder (PTSD)

PTSD criteria are reserved for those older than six years old, and the duration of symptoms is longer than one month with clinically significant distress or impairment observed in social, occupational, or other important areas of functioning (school, for example). There must be exposure to actual or threatened death, serious injury, or sexual violence through directly experiencing or witnessing the event (physical proximity), learning the traumatic event occurred to a close family member or friend (emotional proximity), or experiencing repeated or extreme exposure to details of the traumatic event. However, the DSM-5 explicitly states that exposure to details cannot be solely through electronic media, television, movies, or pictures, unless work-related. This exception is controversial due to the constant access students now have to electronic media and the impact it has on threat perceptions.

There must also be evidence of intrusion symptoms, persistent avoidance of stimuli associated with the trauma, negative alterations in cognitions and mood, and alterations in arousal and reactivity associated with the traumatic event. In addition, the symptoms below also acknowledge the development of maladaptive schemas about one's self, world, and future. These maladaptive schemas lead youth down a pathway of increased psychological risk factors and delinquency (see chapter 4).

PTSD could look like:

Intrusion Symptoms:

- Distressing memories that interfere with ability to concentrate or be comfortable in the environment (for younger children, this can be expressed through repetitive play using trauma themes)
- Acting/feeling as if the event were recurring (flashbacks, reenactment in play)
- Psychological distress at exposure to cues ("trauma triggers") that resemble the traumatic event
- Physiological reactivity to cues that symbolize/resemble the traumatic event (for example, Taylor's body immediately responding to the teacher's voice)
- Recurrent distressing dreams (scary dreams without being able to recognize the content)

Avoidance Symptoms:

- Avoids distressing memories, thoughts, or feelings and/or external reminders (activities, situations, people, places, conversations, objects) that arouse distressing memories, thoughts, or feelings
- Constricted play or social withdrawal

Negative alterations in cognitions and mood:

- Inability to remember an important aspect of the event

- Negative beliefs or expectations about self, life, and others: "I am bad." "I can't trust anyone." "I'll never be happy again."
- Blame self about cause or consequence of the event
- Persistent negative emotions (fear, anger, guilt, shame)
- Diminished interest/participation in significant activities
- Feelings of detachment or estrangement (don't feel emotionally connected to or accepted by friends)
- Distrust and defiance
- Inability to experience positive emotions

Increased Arousal Symptoms:

- Irritability or outbursts of anger/aggression without provocation (verbally or physically lashing out at teachers and friends; extreme temper tantrums)
- Reckless/self-destructive behaviors (excessive drinking, driving at high rates of speed, putting self in unsafe situations)
- Hypervigilance (noticing noises and sounds others are able to ignore)
- Exaggerated startle response
- Difficulty concentrating
- Difficulty falling or staying asleep

It is important to note that many youths may only meet criteria for a partial diagnosis of PTSD, as they may turn to substance use and suicidal ideation as a way to cope, thus masking the symptoms.

DSM-5 added new criteria titled "PTSD for Children Six Years and Younger." While the requirements and symptoms are consistent with those mentioned above, the DSM-5 provides more developmentally appropriate examples. Symptoms in this age group often occur in dreams (content of the dreams may be frightening, but without recognizable content), reactions such as flashbacks may manifest as trauma-specific reenactment play, and feelings of detachment are replaced with social withdrawal.

Acute Stress Disorder

Acute Stress Disorder also involves direct or indirect exposure to actual or threatened death, serious injury, or sexual violation, and also includes the electronic media exception. However, the symptoms are immediately observed, are more severe than common reactions, and persist for at least three days and up to a month with clinically significant distress and impairment observed.

At school, ASD could look like:

- So overwhelmed the student completely shuts down
- Struggles to start or complete simple tasks
- Highly anxious and scared which impacts ability to function
- Refuses to leave the home and come to school
- Refuses to go to sleep for fear of nightmares, thus may fall asleep in class
- Evidence of intrusion, dissociative, avoidance, and arousal symptoms, and/or negative mood associated with the traumatic event similar to what is outlined above in PTSD

It is important to note that an individual does not have to be diagnosed with Acute Stress Disorder in order to be diagnosed with PTSD, and vice versa.

Adjustment Disorder

Adjustment Disorder involves the development of emotional or behavioral response to an identifiable stressor occurring within three months of the stressor onset. The distress is out of proportion to the severity and intensity of the stressor (taking into account cultural factors and norms), and significant impairment is observed in areas of functioning. The symptoms are related to normal bereavement, do not meet the criteria for another mental disorder, and once the stressor is over, the symptoms do not persist for more than six months.

While trauma-related disorders are often formally diagnosed by a qualified mental health professional or medical professional, school mental health professionals are critical to recognizing the signs and symptoms and referring primary caregivers to well-trained professionals who can appropriately diagnose and recommend treatment options. If parents are willing to sign a release of information, school professionals can and should work collaboratively with mental health and medical professionals to ensure treatment and intervention efforts are coordinated. A student may also be referred to the Student Assistance Team and benefit from additional services within the school.

A Student's Story

Maliah can't stop thinking about the storm. Her brain keeps replaying the experience over and over again. The dark, ominous clouds approached, the winds began to pick up, and then it went eerily quiet. All of a sudden, the windows started rattling, the house was shaking, and her parents and siblings had a look of horror on their faces as they were huddled in a bathroom with a mattress over their heads. Winds exceeded one hundred miles per hour and objects in the house began to fall to the ground and shatter. Her sibling were crying hysterically.

Ever since her family's home was damaged by the tornado, she cannot stop thinking about it. She hears the sounds and sees the sights, just like it is happening again. It's been four months, but any sound of thunder, signs of dark clouds, noises of heavy winds, or forecasts of heavy rain send her into an anxiety attack. She refuses to go to school and will hide under objects and refuse to come out. Her body and brain go into "flight" mode. Learning feels impossible.

QUESTIONS to CONSIDER

1. What trauma symptoms is Maliah exhibiting?

2. Are these symptoms consistent with ASD, PTSD, or adjustment disorder?

3. Could Maliah qualify for additional supports and services at school?

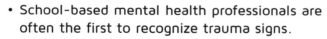

KEY POINTS

- School-based mental health professionals are often the first to recognize trauma signs.

- Severe trauma reactions and associated behaviors may qualify a student for additional supports in school (i.e. a 504 Plan or Individualized Education Plan-IEP).

- It's important to understand the distinction between common reactions, PTSD, acute stress disorder, and adjustment disorder for accurate identification and treatment.

4 Is It Misbehavior or Trauma-Related?

Jennifer has been suspended multiple times. She is oppositional, disrespectful, sarcastic, and often interprets others' intentions as hostile, which leads to physical fighting. At times, she refuses to attend school, engages in daily use of marijuana, and has run away from home and placements outside of the home. She can withdraw, but mostly she externalizes her behaviors. She has alternated between engagement and disengagement with mental health treatment, appears to have disrupted attachment, and has been removed from her home. She has also been arrested for shoplifting. Her mother has substance abuse issues and her father is incarcerated with a long history of domestic violence in the home. Teachers report she is bright when she applies herself, but she is so angry most days that her teachers have given up on trying to connect with her. Now they just want her out of their classroom so she can no longer disrupt the learning environment for others.

> *"Traumatized students are often focused on survival, which hampers their ability to learn, socialize, and develop the skills needed to thrive."*
>
> —Rossen and Cowan
> "The Role of Schools in Supporting Traumatized Students"[13]

It is not uncommon for students with trauma histories to be misunderstood and misidentified. The intervention and programming decisions made based on a misdiagnosis can alter the trajectory of a student's life. If diagnosed as oppositional-defiant disorder or conduct disorder, the intervention pathway is often suspension, expulsion, or an alternative education program. If diagnosed as trauma-based, then special education and/or mental health supports are often engaged with a stronger focus on keeping them engaged in an academic setting with specialized programming.

In their work entitled "Re-examining conduct disorder through the lens of complex trauma," Jessica Linnick and colleagues studied adolescents adjudicated into the juvenile justice system. Sixty percent of those with behavior problems had more than two ACEs; high rates of trauma exposure were found in youth diagnosed with conduct disorder; polyvictimization increased the likelihood of conduct disorder; and maltreatment predicted adult arrests for violent offenses.[14] In addition, young people with PTSD and conduct disorder symptoms demonstrated the following:

- impaired emotional processing, often associated with aggressive behavior and poor social functioning
- misinterpretation of social cues conveyed through facial expressions; those diagnosed with conduct disorders tended to be hypersensitive to fear
- high reactivity to negative emotional stimuli (increased activity in the amygdala)
- difficulty with cognitively controlling emotional responses and response inhibition
- problems with selective and sustained attention
- did not respond as well to positive and negative reinforcement or punishment

While it may appear that behaviors are willful disobedience or defiance, the trauma brain and body can unconsciously react. Behaviors must be screened through the trauma lens.

Conduct disorder describes the behaviors;
trauma-related symptoms help provide their etiology.

Trauma-related disorders are not the only consequence of trauma exposure. Other disorders share comorbidity with PTSD. Thus, it is critical for school mental health professionals to be knowledgeable of associated symptoms and diagnoses. The chart below summarizes the most common overlapping symptoms observed in school-aged, trauma-exposed youth.

ASSOCIATED DISABILITY/ DISORDER	OVERLAPPING TRAUMA SYMPTOMS & BEHAVIORS
Depression	Interpersonal difficulties Withdrawal Decreased affect regulation Cognitively disorganized

Learning Disability	Decreased attention and focus
	Difficulties:
	    concentrating
	    processing instructions and multi-step directions
	    problem-solving
	    understanding consequences of actions
	    paying attention to detail
	Reduced executive functions

ADHD	Impulsive reaction/defense response to stimuli/perceived threat
	Doesn't seem to listen when spoken to directly
	Difficulties:
	    following through on instructions and failure to finish work
	    organizing
	Avoids tasks that require sustained effort
	Forgetful

Anxiety Disorders	Heightened vigilance Self-protective behaviors (aggression, withdrawal, avoidance)
Emotional Disability	Inaccurate perception or interpretation of danger (e.g. judges things as scary/dangerous when they are not)
Mood Disorders (i.e. Bipolar Disorder)	Inconsistent moods Easily upset
Oppositional Defiant Disorder	Angry/irritable Easily annoyed Argues with authority figures Refuses to comply with requests Behaviors are associated with distress in environment
Conduct Disorder	Aggression Lies or deceitfulness Difficulties following rules Unconcerned about performance Shows little emotion and/or empathy
Developmental Disorders	Failure to thrive

Obsessive-Compulsive Disorder	Rigidity and perfectionism
Substance Abuse Disorders	Significant use of substances (i.e. "self-medicating")
Specific Phobias	Significant and persistent fear of specific situations or objects

Many of these students struggle with academics due to gaps in their learning. To mask these difficulties, they will often act out in front of their peers. They would much rather look like the bad kid than the stupid kid.

Attachment

Linnick and colleagues also studied trauma through the lens of attachment theory.[15] So what does that have to do with trauma? A lot actually. Attachment is the deep and enduring emotional bond that connects one person to another. It is adaptive and necessary for survival and the development of healthy emotional regulation and relationships. Healthy attachment helps us to modulate and regulate the experience of negative emotions by recognizing rules and predicting others' behaviors; it promotes the experience of positive emotions; and it helps develop the capacity to regulate arousal and form a healthy bond with others. The caregiver's responsibility is to respond sensitively to the child's needs and help the child learn to manage difficult emotions. For those with trauma histories, their ability to emotionally attach to and trust others has often been compromised.

Attachment is categorized into four types:

Secure attachment is when the caregiver and child have a healthy emotional bond based upon trust and physical and emotional needs are met. While the child shows some stress when the primary caregiver leaves, the adult is perceived as a stable support, making it okay for the child to explore their independence, and the child knows the caregiver will be there when they return. This type of attachment is seen as a protective factor against trauma and later psychopathology and personality disorders.

Anxious/preoccupied attachment is when the child has been anxiously attached to their attachment figure and has difficulties coping with separation. They overreact to the anticipation of or actual separation from their attachment figure. The anxiety comes from the intense and/or unstable relationship which heightens anxiety and feeling emotionally overwhelmed. This style of attachment leads to a reactive autonomic nervous system (primary mechanism in control of the fight-or-flight response). Thus, the child exhibits high levels of emotional expressiveness, worry, and impulsiveness in their relationships, and they are sensitive to rejection. They also seek attention by any means and have a strong desire to fit in and be accepted by others. This can lead to self-sabotaging behaviors and a negative view of self.

Avoidant/Dismissing attachment is when a parent does just that with their children. They avoid them or dismiss their needs. This type of parent minimizes their child's concerns, is emotionally unavailable, has a hard time identifying emotions of their child, and lacks interest in and a desire to form emotional attachments with their child. A child with this type of attachment deliberately acts out or breaks rules, or they indulge in self-destructive behaviors during the teenage years. They can also become high achievers to try and gain acceptance by their caregiver. As they emerge into later adolescents and adulthood, they are more left-brain (logical) and their sense of identity is invested in their abilities or accomplishments, which are often embedded in a high/overly inflated sense of self-esteem. However, underneath they are sensitive to negative feedback from others and will distance themselves from relationships where they are becoming too close or the other person provides honest feedback they don't want to hear.

Fearful-avoidant (disorganized) attachment involves parents who respond to their child's needs in threatening ways or who are unable to care for and comfort their child. This is often the result of severe (oftentimes long-term) childhood trauma, emotional neglect, or abuse. The caregivers may have been physically violent, abusive, suffering from PTSD or personality disorders, or severely depressed. When needing comfort, the child often finds a frightened parent who will scare or confuse them and is unable to soothe them. These interactions impact brain development which changes the sensitivity and emotional regulation of the brain. This leads to the child vacillating between hyper- and hypo-aroused and being highly emotionally dysregulated. They are difficult to predict, have no coherent strategy of relating to others, can tend to dissociate ("blank out") as a way to cope, and feel uncomfortable with emotional closeness. This leads to suppression of feelings, and they do feel they deserve or are worthy of love, yet they often seek comfort from the person who caused them pain. They do not trust needing another person for fear that they will be rejected.

Survival Coping

Those who have been exposed to trauma or have unhealthy attachment are focused on survival. Earning good grades and following rules they often do not understand (as these are not like the rules in their own home) are not high priorities. While many have developed maladaptive behaviors, they are not born to "be bad." These maladaptive behaviors are shaped by their attachment to their primary caregiver and life experiences and are often used to relieve the anxiety of victimization in order to protect self. Many behaviors activate at the biological level (remember "flipping their lid") and may persist even when no longer necessary. While the survival coping strategies may be adaptive in their home or community environment (e.g. hypervigilance, fight or flight when in danger), these same behaviors are seen as maladaptive in the educational setting.

Summary

Students with trauma histories and difficulty with attachment are challenging to teach. They often push adults away and/or respond inconsistently to interventions and supports. For many teachers, this leads to feelings of incompetence because they feel unsuccessful in reaching the student. When school mental health professionals and educators view the student through the trauma and attachment lenses, it helps to better understand and empathize with the student's struggles and lack of trust in adults. Building a trusting relationship takes time, but it is very important to not give up and abandon the student. They have had enough adults do this already. With the right supports and building of SEL skills, relationships can be built and trauma overcome.

A Student's Story

Adam's mother has made it clear she never wanted him. He always feels he is in her way. He was the last-born, a mistake, the one who prevented her from going back to school. She barely engages in anything that has to do with him and she marginalizes his feelings. She tells him to "get over it" when he is unhappy, yet she encourages him to fight for himself, including engaging in physical fighting, if needed. He tries so hard to get his mother's attention and to show her that he is a good and smart son. Nothing has worked.

QUESTIONS to CONSIDER

1. What is the etiology of Adam's behavior?

2. What type of attachment does Adam have with his mother?

3. What additional information would be helpful to provide supports based upon what he needs?

4. What skills can Adam be taught to help him develop positive relationships to at least one trusting adult?

KEY POINTS

- Students with trauma exposure, in particular toxic stress and a higher number of ACEs, are often disruptive at school or will shut down.
- A traumatized brain focuses on survival.
- Behavioral symptoms can mask trauma symptoms.
- Understanding the etiology of the behavior helps ensure the right interventions are implemented to treat the trauma.

How Can Teachers Help Students Exposed to Trauma?

5

The demands placed on teachers are greater today than ever before. Teachers and support staff must receive training on how to identify and better understand trauma. While we don't want teachers thinking they need to become counselors, they are on the frontlines and will notice these behaviors for what they are when others may not. When teachers are "trauma informed" and "trauma sensitive," they can create a classroom atmosphere of emotional and physical safety. A trauma-informed approach includes gentle redirection, confronting with a non-aggressive pose, not taking the situation personally, and focusing on developing trusting relationships; all help to more effectively manage behavior. This approach actually helps all students, regardless of trauma history. This chapter will focus on what teachers can do at the individual and classroom level, then we'll discuss creating a trauma-sensitive school further in chapter 7.

All behavior is telling us something;
changes in behavior have a reason.

Past behavior can be a strong indicator of future behavior,
but it doesn't mean it has to define whom one becomes!

Maslow's Hierarchy of Needs (in the classroom)

Many of us have studied Maslow's hierarchy of needs. A trauma-sensitive classroom must address these needs for students to feel physically and psychologically safe. This graphic demonstrates how the hierarchy is applied to the classroom environment.

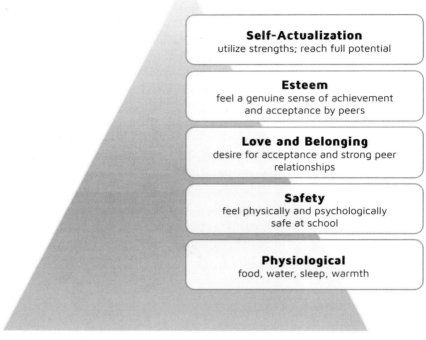

Self-Actualization
utilize strengths; reach full potential

Esteem
feel a genuine sense of achievement and acceptance by peers

Love and Belonging
desire for acceptance and strong peer relationships

Safety
feel physically and psychologically safe at school

Physiological
food, water, sleep, warmth

Source: Adapted from ChangeKidsLives.org[16]

Physiological Needs. Many students with trauma histories (particularly neglect) will not have these needs fully met at home. Thus, it is important for students to have water breaks, access to healthy meals, a place to rest for a period of time if they are physically exhausted (e.g. a power nap), and clothing appropriate for the temperature. For example, food insecurity leads to extreme hunger, which then drops blood sugar, which then leads to students being angry. Can the school provide breakfast, as this also provides fuel for the brain to think better?

Safety. This encompasses both physical and psychological safety. Physical safety includes trying to address/minimize ongoing stressors and keeping the school day as safe as possible.

Practicing emergency protocols helps gain a sense of control, thus helping to mitigate traumatic impact. (Do not conduct highly sensorial active-shooter drills that involve alarm sounds, screaming, or fake gun shots! This is traumatizing!) Psychological safety includes involving the students in establishing clear classroom expectations for behavior, collaborative and supportive problem-solving to create a classroom of trust, acceptance for all that is free from bullying, and an environment where differences are celebrated.

Nobody wants to be tolerated. They want to be accepted.

Love and Belonging. To facilitate strong peer relationships, teachers should periodically change the seating arrangement, group students who lack friends with those who are friendly and accepting, and utilize collaborative projects that build upon each student's strengths. Sharing is encouraged. Be prepared to guide a student through a trauma trigger or episode of intense emotion and facilitate reintegration into the classroom. Also be sure to offer unconditional positive regard and ask what they need.

Esteem. Integrate social-emotional learning (SEL) lessons that focus on developing internal and external resiliency and a strong sense of self and self-identity. Internal resiliency includes promoting active (or approach-oriented) coping styles, promoting an internal locus of control, championing student mental health, and teaching students how to better regulate their emotions. This can be done by teaching skills to include stress and conflict management, decision-making, and problem-solving. Students impacted by trauma can be taught to think about trauma triggers rather than emotionally respond. Positive affirmations provided by the teacher, by the students, and to each other are a must and there should be at least seven positive comments to one negative/redirection comment! In addition, social-emotional skills should be rewarded, not just academic skills.

External resiliency is built by facilitating school connectedness and engagement, supporting families (i.e., provide parent education and appropriate social services), facilitating peer relationships, providing access to positive adult role models, and ensuring connections with pro-social institutions/activities.

> **"Resiliency—It's not something you are born with. It's something that is built over time."**
> — Dr. Jack Shonkoff [17]

Self-Actualization. This is when students feel successful both academically and socially. This is not about being the highest achieving student in the class; it is about making progress and showing growth. Students feel comfortable in who they are and are able to identify and use their strengths. Teachers help students reach this highest level by providing many opportunities and ways to demonstrate success.

Classroom Structure

A trauma-sensitive classroom focuses on resilience, maintains high academic standards and expectations, promotes opportunities for success, and monitors and installs intrinsic rewards for student progress. Flexibility, predictability, engagement, and communication are key.

> **Always empower but never disempower.**

Flexibility to accommodate emotional space. A trauma-sensitive classroom provides structure, consistency, and predictability yet also offers flexibility to accommodate the student's "emotional space." For example, two students begin to have a disagreement, which serves as a trauma trigger for Johnny as the domestic violence in his home often begins with small disagreements. He freezes, his heart is racing, and his mind goes blank. It's now lunch time and his worksheet is not done. When the teacher directs students to submit their assignments to her on their way to lunch, he crosses his arms and places his hands on his shoulders. Unknown to other students, this is the signal he and the teacher have discreetly agreed upon that tells the teacher he is overwhelmed and needs space. The teacher quietly offers Johnny choices. He can finish during lunch, finish at the end of the day during silent work time, or take the assignment home and bring it back completed in the morning. He nods his head and whispers he would like to complete it the end of the day. He joins his friends for lunch. This flexible approach avoided a power struggle and allowed Johnny to feel safe communicating his emotional and academic needs to his teacher.

Constructivist approach. This approach engages students to be active participants in their own learning. This facilitates students having a sense of control and minimizes learned helplessness. It also builds a sense of confidence in trying new things and taking academic risks.

Discovery of competence. The learning environment focuses on students' assets (strength-based) so they can discover their own competencies. Trauma victims often do not have the internal control required to engaged in independent inquiry or they are afraid they will fail or do it wrong. Facilitation from an adult is critical to help them explore their own personal strengths with a focus on wellness, not pathology.

Madeline Hunter's Lesson Plan Model. This is an excellent way to teach all students, as this leads to predictable and consistent routines. Madeline Hunter's model of teaching a lesson involves beginning with an anticipatory set to grab the students' attention and gain the arousal necessary for learning, clearly explains the goals and objectives of the lesson (sets the structure and predictability for students), provides input (e.g. vocabulary, links to prior knowledge) and modeling, and then checks for understanding/mastery. Guided practice is followed by independent practice, and the lesson concludes by bridging newly learned knowledge to future learning.

Cooperative learning. Use social skills modeling and group activities to encourage self-differentiation, collaboration, diversity in thought, and application of Social and Emotional Learning (SEL) skills.

Listen. Approach calmly. If the student is escalating, the adult should be deescalating. If able, be eye level with the student while also maintaining an arm's length distance. Relax your body language and speak in a calm voice. Ask them to tell you "what happened" and give them time to share their perspective. Use open-ended questions and avoid lecture-mode or trying to convince; instead model active listening and problem solving.

> **Students with trauma histories are sensitive to personal space and firm voice tones.**
>
> **If a teacher approaches with firm demands and/or invades the student's personal space, these could serve as trauma triggers.**

Academic Interventions

Below are interventions to address specifics areas of executive functioning needed for classroom success:

Promote Initiation/Focus

- Structure: When a child experiences trauma, we tend to "loosen" the structure for a period of time because we "feel sorry" for the student. Structure that is consistent and predictable is critical while also allowing for flexibility to accommodate emotional space.
- Consistent and predictable daily routines: Routines help form habits, as predictability decreases anxiety.
- Short breaks and activities: These increase students' overall level of arousal and energy level.
- External prompting (cues, oral directions): Prompting orients the child to the fact that initiation is required and increases attention.
- Allow time for self-engagement: Providing a warning before transition, or providing choices instead of expecting immediate compliance, prevents power struggles.
- Provide daily quiet time: Quiet time helps students "re-center" and decompress.

- Provide a "fidget box" or a "calm box" with small items: Holding an item helps students feel more relaxed and focused.
- Use a "calming space" or "safe space" for students to relax and decompress: Calming spaces help students regulate their emotions.

Facilitate Memory

- Shorten multi-step directions: Ask the child to repeat the directions.
- Post the directions on the board or in the classroom.
- Provide visual aids: Teachers who "lecture" are not good matches; students need multi-modal styles of teaching/ presenting new material.
- Use visualization or "seeing" the information as a teaching strategy.
- Allow students to take pictures of the board to facilitate delayed recall.

Inhibition (resistance to act upon first impulse)

- Model, teach, and practice mental routines that encourage the child to stop and think: Stop! Think. Good choice? Bad Choice?
- Allow them to write, draw, and color to express emotion.
- Examine situations/environments to identify antecedent conditions that will trigger disinhibited behavior: Alter those conditions. When students feel unsafe or threatened, they tend to act out or "retaliate."
  - o Engage your school psychologist who has specialized training in conducting a functional behavioral assessment (FBA).
- Post positively stated rules and expectations in the classroom: Informs students of the limits of acceptable behavior.
- Provide specific guidance on what to do, instead of focusing on what not to do.

Self-Monitoring

- Model, teach, and practice use of monitoring routines: i.e. Proofread written work using the C.O.P.S. method: Capitalization, Organization, Punctuation, and Spelling.
- Use verbal and non-verbal prompts to check for understanding.
- Establish a non-verbal signal the student can give to the teacher when angry, overwhelmed, and/or in need of a break.

Behavioral Regulation

- Integrate SEL lessons into classroom curriculum.
- Help to identify triggers: Remove stimuli that lead to trauma triggers or inappropriate behavior.
- Teach grounding, focusing skills, stretching, movement, relaxation strategies (i.e. mindfulness).
- Add feeling words to spelling lists or language-based tasks: Increases emotional vocabulary.
- Help students understand how their behavior affects others: Balance accountability with understanding of behavior.
- Utilize natural consequences: Use teachable moments. Avoid the use of exclusionary discipline (e.g. detention, suspension, expulsion).
- Anticipate challenges and provide more supports/guidance.
- Facilitate a classroom meeting after a crisis: See Appendix A.

Mindfulness and Cautions

Mindfulness is a fast-growing trend in schools. Students are being taught how to focus their awareness on the present moment by relaxing their bodies using breathing techniques and positive thinking/visualization in order to decrease stress. Teachers are using this technique to restore calm to the classroom, help students find quiet space, and build self-regulation skills. It also helps teachers respond more calmly to students and keep a positive perspective. However, some of the techniques such as sitting still and keeping eyes closed in silence can be a trigger for students who have experienced trauma.

Signs a student may not benefit from or want mindfulness due to having trauma history:

- The activity is not taken seriously.
- The silence is a trauma trigger so they may refuse to participate or act out. The silence can feel like a storm is brewing or "the shoe is going to drop"; they disrupt the activity to avoid the silence.
- The multiple steps are overwhelming and the student feels too many requests are being made of them. Thus, they may act out or refuse to comply.
- Students exhibit avoidance behavior.

Guidelines for teachers using mindfulness when trauma history is present:

1. Don't force it. Give students forewarning, and for those with trauma histories, offer another activity.
2. Don't force them to close their eyes or do other actions they don't want to. They can still benefit from sitting quietly and taking a break.
3. Build relationships as the student must trust the process and the teacher.

Vicarious Trauma and Secondary Traumatic Stress

Teachers (and most all educators) are under tremendous stress. Meeting the needs of trauma exposed students is not easy and does not come without personal sacrifices. Educators and school mental health professionals need to be aware of signs of distress within themselves. Below is a summary of the secondary effects of this work:

Burnout	emotional exhaustion, depersonalization, sense of reduced personal accomplishment; result of general occupational stress
Compassion fatigue	physical and mental exhaustion, emotional withdrawal, apathy and/or indifference toward the suffering of others due to the exposure of caring for those impacted by trauma over time
Secondary Traumatic Stress (STS)	experiencing emotional distress symptoms similar to Post Traumatic Stress Disorder (PTSD) due to hearing about the traumatic experiences of another individual, even though professional was not necessarily exposed to direct trauma themselves
Vicarious traumatization (VT)	internal changes in professionals who engage empathetically with those affected by trauma; more focused on the cumulative effects of exposure to another's trauma details

STS and VT are often used interchangeably as both refer to the indirect trauma symptoms that can occur when exposed to difficult or disturbing images and stories secondhand. Trauma sensitive schools must recognize and support teachers who may be showing signs of VT and STS. Below are the common symptoms of STS:

- increased anxiety and concern about safety
- intrusive, negative thoughts and images related to their students' traumatic stories (e.g. keep reliving/thinking about student's traumatic stories)
- diminished concentration, difficulty with decision making
- fatigue
- physical complaints
- feeling numb or detached from students and work
- feeling powerless or hopeless about students and their work
- desire to physically or emotionally withdraw from people or situations that trigger difficult thoughts and emotions

If supports are not offered, negative impact on personal and professional lives can occur as signaled by the warning signs of VT:

- hypervigilance
- excessive alertness for potential threats or dangers at and outside of work (e.g. constantly "on the lookout" or "looking over shoulder" for fear something bad is going to happen)
- poor boundaries: difficulties separating work/home life; take too much work home
- unbalanced work life: take on too much, try to control events, take work too personally
- avoidance coping by shutting down and disconnecting or overly engaging in activities to try and avoid negative thoughts/emotions
- inability to empathize
- feel "numb": unable to remain emotionally connected to the work
- self-medicate with drugs/alcohol/substances
- attaching to distractions to check out from work, personal life, or both
- chronic exhaustion
- physical ailments
- physical, emotional, and spiritual fatigue
- minimizing a current experience by comparing it with another situation that is perceived as more severe
- anger and cynicism
- feelings of professional inadequacy; second-guessing self as a professional

Self-Care (a.k.a. "Career Sustaining Behaviors)

Teacher retention and the negative effects of caring for those with trauma exposure can be mitigated by good self-care. Self-care needs to be integrated into the framework of the school's climate and culture and emphasized and modeled by leadership.

If a teacher's stress response system is dysregulated, how can they expect their students to regulate their own?

Below are helpful self-care strategies for all staff:

- educate staff on VT, STS, burnout, and compassion fatigue
- identify social supports
- engage in fun activities, activism, advocacy, and actions that promote healing and laughter
- use creative self-expression (art, poetry)
- employ humor (but don't confuse with sarcasm)
- practice gratitude towards each other
- get adequate sleep
- take breaks during day (e.g. mindfulness; walking around the track) and from work on evenings and weekends
- set boundaries
- eat a healthy and balanced diet
- avoid excessive use of alcohol
- exercise
- employ stress management techniques
- practice faith and spirituality
- reach out for help

By employing personal self-care and encouraging colleagues to do the same, educational professionals can experience *compassion satisfaction*. This is when a professional experiences positive feelings, feels competent, and believes their efforts are contributing in a meaningful way, and where positive relationships with colleagues are formed. When these career sustaining behaviors are formed, a solid foundation for a trauma sensitive school is established.

A Teacher's Story

Mr. Smith is exhausted. His community experienced a wildfire and his home was significantly damaged. He and his family are now living with relatives indefinitely. Many of his students were also displaced. Their behaviors have escalated in the classroom, making teaching very difficult and exhausting. Many families are struggling to find food, so Mr. Smith has volunteered his evenings to deliver food baskets to student families. His principal just announced they are adopting a new curriculum so teachers will need to make time for staff development as academic scores will be closely monitored. While he has loved teaching, he feels the task is becoming impossible. During class one day, students were misbehaving and he lashed out at them. He has never done this before and the kids looked horrified. He was on the verge of "losing it" and is now beginning to wonder if all of this is worth it.

QUESTIONS to CONSIDER

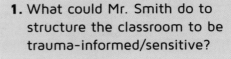

1. What could Mr. Smith do to structure the classroom to be trauma-informed/sensitive?

2. What are the signs and symptoms of STS and VT?

3. What can he do for self-care?

4. What resources are available to Mr. Smith?

5. How can leadership ensure all staff have supports needed?

KEY POINTS

- Modify the classroom structure and instructional approaches to be trauma-informed/sensitive.
- Mindfulness must be used cautiously with those with trauma histories.
- Collaborate with your school mental health professional.
- STS and VT are real. Educators and school mental health professionals must take care of themselves and reach out for supports.
- Leadership must model and support self-care.

How Can School Mental Health Professionals Help Students Exposed to Trauma?

In addition to their direct work with students, school mental health professionals can help teachers implement the strategies identified in chapter 5 and are critical to guiding administrators in establishing a trauma-sensitive school climate and culture that will be discussed in chapter 7. Of the thirty-five million children exposed to trauma, only eight million have access to a school psychologist. And of the general school population, nearly one in five students do not have access to a school counselor.[18] This is a disappointing reality, as oftentimes school mental health professionals are the only mental health professionals students have access to. If we can increase accessibility to school mental health professionals, we can begin to better identify and treat trauma.

Prevention – School Climate and Culture

Overall positive school climate and culture can mitigate the effects of trauma, whereas a negative or dysfunctional culture can add to the cumulative effects of trauma. Prevention programs help to build the protective factors that mitigate the development of trauma reactions. Thus, school mental health professionals need to advocate for and be well-versed in evidenced-based prevention programs, and, more importantly, they must be given the time in their schedules to implement prevention programs. School climates that support traumatized youth include the following:

1. Fully integrated, cohesive approaches to learning supports (e.g., behavioral, mental health, and social services), instruction, and school management that facilitates multidisciplinary collaboration.

2. Multitiered systems of supports (MTSS) that increase with intensity based on student need.

3. Access to supports from school-employed mental health professionals specifically trained to work in schools who have expertise in the integration of social, emotional, academic, and behavioral supports and expertise in parent-school-community collaboration.

4. Integrated and ongoing school climate and safety efforts with crisis prevention through recovery efforts.

5. Effective, positive school discipline that is fair and equitable; reinforcement of positive behaviors, teaching of replacement skills, and restorative practices to support students in making positive changes.

Punishment alone does not change behavior!

6. School-wide social emotional learning curriculum to strengthen internal and external resiliency.

Intervention/Response – Acute Traumatic Stressor

When students are exposed to an acute stressor, crisis interventions and supports must be provided to mitigate traumatic impact.

Psychological First Aid for Schools

Proactively, school mental health professionals can train all school staff in Psychological First Aid (PFA). This is a specific training curriculum that increases knowledge of how to be the "frontline" supports for students. PFA has been shown to reduce the initial distress caused by a crisis event, allow for the expression of crisis related feelings, and assist students in developing coping strategies and adaptive actions.

PFA establishes a positive connection in a non-intrusive, compassionate manner; provides physical and emotional comfort to reaffirm perceptions of safety and security; calms and orients those who are emotionally overwhelmed or distraught; helps to identify (i.e. psychological triage) immediate needs and concerns; offers practical assistance and helpful information; and empowers individuals by acknowledging strengths and adaptive coping efforts. Community resources can also be activated. The six PFA steps are:

1. Clarify trauma facts
2. Normalize reactions
3. Encouraging expression of feelings
4. Provide education to the child about experience
5. Encourage exploration and correction of inaccurate attributions regarding the trauma
6. Stress management strategies

It is important to note that teachers and other support staff do not fulfill the role of the school mental health professional. They serve as the "front lines" to provide basic supports and refer to school mental health professionals when additional school and/or community supports need to be activated.

When exposed to an acute traumatic stressor, the *PREPaRE School Crisis Prevention and Intervention Curriculum* provides a multitiered approach to crisis intervention and supports.[19] The PREPaRE model is the only known comprehensive school-based crisis training model to incorporate a multitiered framework that aligns well with MTSS and other comprehensive school safety and educational approaches and incorporates best practices advocated for by the U.S. Departments of Education and Homeland Security.

The PREPaRE acronym stands for the following:

P	Prevent and prepare for psychological trauma
R	Reaffirm physical health and perceptions of security and safety
E	Evaluate psychological trauma risk
P	Provide interventions
a	and
R	Respond to psychological needs
E	Examine the effectiveness of crisis prevention and intervention

Conducting psychological triage and evaluating for psychological trauma risk is the foundation of providing good quality crisis supports. The PREPaRE model emphasizes that *multitiered* crisis supports offered should be based upon demonstrated need. Some individuals may need highly directive crisis intervention supports, whereas for others, natural support systems will be sufficient. A one-size-fits-all approach (e.g. opening up a room and having teachers send students down) should be avoided. This can lead to vicarious traumatization, students seeking help who don't really need it or just want to get out of class, and students who need support may be missed if we wait for them to come down.

Below (and in Appendix B) is a summary of multi-tiered crisis interventions according to the PREPaRE model.

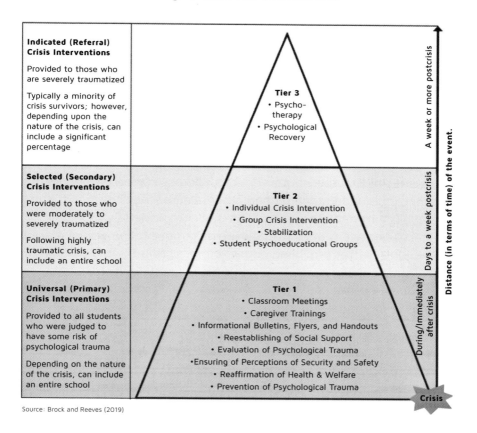

Indicated (Referral) Crisis Interventions

Provided to those who are severely traumatized

Typically a minority of crisis survivors; however, depending upon the nature of the crisis, can include a significant percentage

Selected (Secondary) Crisis Interventions

Provided to those who were moderately to severely traumatized

Following highly traumatic crisis, can include an entire school

Universal (Primary) Crisis Interventions

Provided to all students who are judged to have some risk of psychological trauma

Depending on the nature of the crisis, can include an entire school

Tier 3
- Psycho-therapy
- Psychological Recovery

Tier 2
- Individual Crisis Intervention
- Group Crisis Intervention
- Stabilization
- Student Psychoeducational Groups

Tier 1
- Classroom Meetings
- Caregiver Trainings
- Informational Bulletins, Flyers, and Handouts
- Reestablishing of Social Support
- Evaluation of Psychological Trauma
- Ensuring of Perceptions of Security and Safety
- Reaffirmation of Health & Welfare
- Prevention of Psychological Trauma

A week or more postcrisis | Days to a week postcrisis | During/Immediately after crisis

Distance (in terms of time) of the event.

Crisis

Source: Brock and Reeves (2019)

Tier 1: Universal Crisis Interventions

Tier 1 interventions are offered to all crisis-exposed individuals and are designed to prevent or mitigate psychological trauma and reaffirm physical health and perceptions of safety and security. Evaluating psychological trauma (psychological triage) helps to ensure that appropriate interventions are provided. Tier 1 supports include reaffirming perceptions of safety and security, reestablishing social support systems, providing basic psychoeducational information, conducting classroom meetings (see sample script in Appendix A) to share the facts and letting students know how and where to find additional supports, if needed, and conducting caregiver training for staff and parents.

Tier 2: Selected/Targeted/Secondary Crisis Interventions

Tier 2 crisis interventions are more prescriptive and directive supports only offered to those who are moderately to severely traumatized. Tier 2 interventions are typically administered shortly after the crisis event (i.e., a few days to a couple of weeks) with the goal of helping students understand why they are reacting as they are. Interventions at this level include student psychoeducational groups, group crisis intervention, and individual crisis intervention. More specifically, these interventions address coping challenges, facilitate the understanding and processing of their reactions, and reestablish immediate coping. This is accomplished by providing practical safety tips and strategies to help make the ongoing stressor more controllable, providing education regarding the biological and brain reactions (i.e. hyperarousal; "upstairs and downstairs brain"), and educating students on the symptoms of traumatic stress so they can seek additional support for self or others if struggling.

Tier 3: Intensive/Indicated/Tertiary Crisis Interventions

Tier 3 interventions are offered to those most severely traumatized. Typically, these are provided at least a week or more after the event (students need time to work through common reactions before activating more directive supports) and include intensive and long-term mental health treatment (i.e. post-traumatic stress disorder). These services often require the engagement of more directive and specialized mental health interventions listed below and/or a referral to services outside the school setting. This may include systems of care or wraparound services described in chapter 8.

Intervention/Response – Toxic/Chronic Stressors

While the interventions highlighted above can be helpful to those experiencing toxic/chronic stress, they oftentimes are insufficient in meeting their trauma needs.

Group-Delivered Cognitive-Behavioral Interventions

The effectiveness of group interventions has been proven effective. The benefits of group approaches in schools include assisting a large number of students at once, decreasing a sense of hopelessness, and normalizing reactions.

One of the most common group-delivered CBT interventions designed for schools is **CBITS (Cognitive Behavioral Interventions for Trauma in Schools)**. This manualized treatment has shown decreases in overall severity of post-traumatic stress symptoms and behavior problems.

CBITS has three primary goals:

1. Decrease current symptoms related to trauma exposure
2. Build skills to handle stress and anxiety
3. Build peer and caregiver supports.

CBITS incorporates the following cognitive-behavioral techniques:

- psychoeducation about trauma and its consequences
- relaxation training
- examining the link between feelings and behaviors; recognizing, challenging, and restructuring maladaptive thinking
- creating trauma narratives and processing the event
- learning to monitor stress and anxiety levels
- facing trauma-related anxieties rather than avoiding them
- social problem-solving skills

CBITS includes ten group sessions, one to three individual sessions, two caregiver education sessions, and one educational presentation for teachers. For more information, visit https://cbitsprogram.org/.

Support for Students Exposed to Trauma (SSET) is an adaptation of CBITS but excludes the individual and parent sessions. The curriculum includes 10 structured lessons aimed at reducing PTSD, depressive symptoms, and deficits in functioning for students who have been exposed to trauma. For more information, visit https://ssetprogram.org/.

Bounce Back is an adaptation of CBITS for K-5 students. The program includes 10 group sessions, 1-3 group parent sessions, and 2-3 individual student sessions. Group session content includes coping skills, feelings identification, relaxation exercises, positive activities, social support, problem solving, and the individual session focuses on developing the trauma narrative. For more information, visit https://bouncebackprogram.org/.

Trauma-Focused Cognitive Behavioral Therapy (TF-CBT) applies traditional CBT strategies. It is considered a components-based program that teaches children and parents stress management skills and encourages direct discussion and processing of children's traumatic experiences by helping the child think about the event using gradual exposure techniques. An emphasis is placed on identification and expression of feelings; relaxation and coping skills training; recognition of the relationship between thoughts, feelings, and behaviors; cognitive processing of experiences; and joint child–parent sessions.

Results show that TF-CBT reduces symptoms of PTSD, depression, and behavior problems immediately after and twelve months following treatment completion. For more information, visit https://tfcbt.org/.

TF-CBT can also incorporate grief-focused components for children suffering from traumatic grief (Cognitive Behavioral Therapy for Childhood Traumatic Grief, CBT-CTG). CBT-CTG consists of sixteen treatment sessions (twelve individual sessions for parents and children and four joint parent–child sessions). The first lessons are trauma-focused, with the latter being grief-focused. Studies have shown decreased PTSD, traumatic grief, and depressive symptoms.

In summary, treating PTSD involves addressing the emotional and interpersonal difficulties to restore a sense of power and control. Survivors are also empowered by healing relationships which create a sense of safety, allow for remembrance and mourning, and promote reconnection with everyday life activities.

A Student's Story

Magdalena thought she was doing well with her recovery after her friend's suicide. After all, it had been four months and shouldn't she be moving forward by now? But a second suicide of a classmate has sent her into a tailspin. She can't stop thinking about it, is having trouble eating and sleeping, doesn't want to go to school, and is constantly worried about the safety of her other friends. She doesn't know what to do but she knows she can't go on like this, and her classmates are struggling too.

QUESTIONS to CONSIDER

1. What are the signs of enduring crisis reactions?

2. What interventions and supports could be provided to Magdalena both inside and outside of school?

3. What individual and group interventions could be provided to help her classmates cope?

KEY POINTS

- School mental health professionals are critical to the establishment of trauma-sensitive schools and high-quality crisis interventions and supports.
- SEL programs build protective factors that can mitigate traumatic impact.
- School mental health professionals can train school staff in PFA and should also be trained themselves in how to deliver multitiered crisis interventions.
- An MTSS approach should be used to provide crisis supports after trauma exposure.
- School mental heath professionals can and should deliver mental health interventions to those with trauma exposure.

How Can Administrators Help Students Exposed to Trauma?

Administrators set the tone for school climate, collaboration, and behavior management. They are critical to establishing a trauma-sensitive school climate where supports and guidance are emphasized, not punishment. Too often administrators (and teachers) end up in power struggles with students because they treated behavior as oppositional or defiant instead of taking the time to figure out what is really underneath the behavior.

"The presence of a supportive relationship is more critical than the absence of ACEs in promoting well-being."

—Documentary, Resilience:
The Biology of Stress & the Science of Hope[20]

Administrators also set priorities. The Collaborative for Academic, Social, and Emotional Learning (CASEL) has shown through years of research that when social-emotional-learning (SEL) is integrated into the academic curriculum, achievement scores are higher and there is a decrease in behavioral challenges.[21] SEL helps students and adults understand and manage emotions; feel and show empathy for others; establish and maintain positive relationships; set and achieve positive goals; and make responsible decisions—all skills critical for academic and life success! By establishing and supporting a strong SEL focus in their school, administrators are building protective factors that mitigate traumatic impact. A school with a strong SEL focus will "weather the trauma storm" much more effectively and return to academic instruction sooner than a school where SEL skills and relationships have not been developed.

The Ongoing Universal Response to Chronic Trauma and Toxic Stress

Trauma-Informed Approach

Students learn best when they feel safe, connected, and supported. The trauma-informed approach is a multitiered framework that aligns with existing multitiered educational practices. Thus, this is not "one more new program," but, instead, it integrates mental health programming into the educational environment. While designed to use in schools where there is a large percentage of students with a trauma exposure or ongoing chronic trauma and toxic stress, it can help *all* students.

This approach embraces a shared understanding and ownership among all staff to support students to feel safe physically, socially, emotionally, and academically. The school addresses students' needs in holistic ways and values relationships, self-regulation, academic competence, and physical and emotional well-being. Multiple opportunities are provided to practice newly developing skills. School professionals facilitate student and family connectedness and *all* staff share responsibility for all students. This is not a "special education student" or "your student," but this is *our* student. Everyone has the mindset of "How can I help?" Leadership and staff also adapt to the ever-changing needs of students.

Creating Trauma-Informed Schools

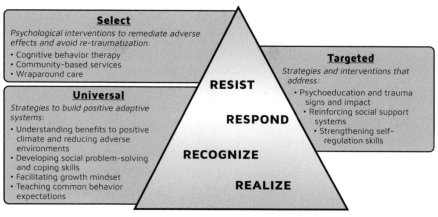

Source: "Toward a Blueprint for Trauma-Informed Service Delivery in Schools"[22]

While more rigorous research is needed, multiple studies show a trauma-informed approach shows an *increase* in academic achievement and test scores, school climate, teacher sense of satisfaction and retention, graduation rates, and community and family collaboration and a *decrease* in student behavioral outbursts and referrals, staff and student stress, absences, detentions, suspensions, and drop-out rates, student bullying, harassment, and fights, and the need for special education services and classes.

The trauma informed approach embraces four key assumptions:

1. All staff realize the widespread impact of trauma and understand potential paths for recovery.

    This is accomplished by hiring teachers and support staff who are invested in learning about trauma and how trauma affects student learning. They are willing to help students through difficult situations (instead of just punishing) and realize that while trauma can explain the behavior, it does not have to define the student's future; thus, positive changes can take place over time with the right supports and guidance.

To help assess staff readiness to embrace the trauma-informed approach, there is the ARTIC – Attitudes Related to Trauma-Informed Care scale (found at: http://traumaticstressinstitute.org/artic-scale/). This scale assesses the extent to which staff attitudes are consistent with trauma-informed approaches and can be used as an initial indicator of staff readiness for a system shift to trauma-informed approaches. It can also be used to monitor changes in staff attitudes in response to professional development to ensure forward moving implementation and sustainability.

2. All staff recognize signs and symptoms of trauma.

Research has shown higher numbers of adverse family experiences are correlated with higher numbers of mental health diagnoses, which correlates with higher school disengagement, grade retention, and qualification for special education services (for example, IEP). To avoid these negative outcomes, a trauma informed staff views behavior through the "trauma lens" as described in chapter 1. Instead of reacting themselves (which creates power struggles), staff and administration implement trauma-informed strategies to deescalate the situation and guide the student to use their SEL skills. Universal screening can maximize detection of students at risk for adverse outcomes, allowing schools to proactively respond with prevention programming and supports. It also helps administrators advocate for school mental health staffing to meet these needs.

3. All staff respond by fully integrating knowledge into policies, procedures, and practices.

Administrators must dedicate time to professional development training that creates shared understanding of the trauma exposure, builds consensus for trauma-informed approaches, and embraces attitudes, beliefs, and behaviors that allow for the adoption and integration of system-wide trauma-informed approaches. Schools (and districts) are notorious for "one-shot" trainings where they conduct a one-time workshop but have no follow-up or sustainability plan. The trauma-informed approach requires a multi-year, ongoing commitment that can withstand the changes of administration and budgets. It is the school culture!

4. All staff seek to actively resist re-traumatization.

   How a staff member approaches a student when there is misbehavior can humiliate, hurt, or heal. Yet, the adaptations a student must make when triggered into the "trauma world" can make students seem bad, unmotivated, hostile, or lost, which then leaves teachers and administrators asking, "What is wrong with this student?'" This type of lens often increases the likelihood of re-traumatization, resulting in punitive disciplinary responses that often include seclusion, change of placement, or harsh zero-tolerance policies. The trauma-informed approach embraces culturally responsive discipline practices and teaches staff members to deescalate the situation and instead ask the student what happened.

"What's wrong with you?" ➡ "Tell me what happened?"

This shifts the conversation to one of willingness to understand the student's perspective and their interpretation of the series of events, which then leads to supportive, problem-solving interventions that avoid re-traumatization. This also allows for the application of SEL skills and helps students learn to differentiate between skills developed at home from the skills it takes to navigate the academic setting. Survival skills needed at home may be counterproductive in the school setting.

Research has also shown the trauma-informed approach helps reduce racial disparities in academic outcomes and suspensions. Thus, if a punitive consequence is warranted, it must be done with care. Not only does this avoid re-traumatization, but it also prevents escalation of negative feelings and grievances.

Response to an Acute Traumatic Stressor

It's not if a crisis will occur, but when. All schools will experience an acute crisis such as a car accident, suicide, or death of a teacher due to long-term illness. Thus, administrators need to be sure they have a well-developed Emergency Operations Plan (EOP) and a well-trained crisis response team, as their leadership helps shape traumatic event perceptions during and after a crisis. A well-developed reunification protocol is also critically important to avoiding adding another trauma on top of the initial trauma due to a chaotic reunification process. Administrators must also be ready to remove staff from a caretaking role if they are emotionally overwhelmed (showing emotions is okay, but losing emotional control and elevating student threat perceptions is not). Good communication and supports to primary caregivers also help mitigate the development of traumatic stress. The PREPaRE Workshop 1: *Crisis Prevention & Preparedness* trains school safety and crisis teams in how to build a good emergency operations plan that addresses the skills mentioned above.[23] Administrators also need to ensure their school mental health professionals receive the appropriate training to deliver multitiered crisis interventions and counseling supports described in chapter 6.

A culturally responsive, trauma-informed school includes the following:

- Psychologically safe school environment
- Increases resilience among school personnel to use open communication, growth, and learning to develop a common language to discuss trauma and concerns
- Honors students and staff identities

- Focuses on appreciation of multiple perspectives
- Makes each interaction meaningful and builds partnerships to support emotional growth
- Focuses on "unpacking the invisible backpack" so trauma is addressed as part of comprehensive programming— increases effective classroom-based strategies
- Family engagement
- Culturally responsive discipline practices

Barriers to implementing trauma-informed services have included:

- Lack of support from administrators/teachers
- Competing teacher responsibilities
- Problems engaging parents
- Stigma regarding mental health concerns
- Cultural/linguistic barriers

Administrators cannot do all this work alone! Thus, they need to advocate for expanding and prioritizing school-based mental health services. It really does take a village to do this work, and school psychologists, school counselors, and school social workers are critical partners!

An Administrator's Story

Raul was sitting outside Principal Jackson's office for the third time this week. Raul threw a chair, refused to talk to the teacher, and threatened to punch another student if he was not left alone. The teacher was at a loss as to how to manage Raul and was insisting he be removed from the class. Raul was scared, as he was being bullied by this other student but he was not going to show he was weak in front of his peers. Principal

Jackson sat down with Raul and asked him to take a few deep breaths (the school counselor had been teaching students stress management strategies as part of the health curriculum). Principal Jackson then opened up the conversation with, "Tell me what happened." Raul proceeded to tell him his perspective and confided that the other student had been bullying him.

QUESTIONS to CONSIDER

1. What were Raul's fears and triggers to his behavior?

2. How could Principal Jackson support his teacher?

3. What needs to be addressed in regards to school culture and possible prevention programming?

4. What other professionals could help Principal Jackson support Raul and his teachers?

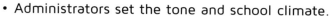

KEY POINTS

- Administrators set the tone and school climate.
- School mental health professionals are critical partners.
- Implementing a trauma-informed, sensitive, and culturally responsive approach builds protective factors.
- Implement SEL and consequences with care. This builds relationships.
- Support staff development to increase trauma-informed skills sets.
- Use your mental health staff for service delivery, not paperwork!

What If a Student Needs More Support?

8

For students without trauma histories, and those whose trauma exposure is mitigated by resiliency and supports, recovery is the norm. Thus, school crisis interventions (such as those delivered according to the PREPaRE model) are sufficient. For acute traumatic stressors that involve violence or a violent death and/or exposure to chronic trauma and toxic stress, school crisis interventions are helpful but often insufficient. Thus, collaboration and partnerships with community mental health providers and agencies is critical.

Cognitive-Behavioral Therapies to Address Trauma

In regards to therapeutic approaches, cognitive behavioral approaches have proven empirical support for the treatment of trauma. Chapter 6 described CBT interventions appropriate for schools. This chapter will provide a brief overview of trauma-focused strategies often used by mental health clinicians outside of schools. School mental health professionals are critical to helping families access these services from qualified professionals.

Exposure Therapies

Exposure therapies are techniques that involve in vivo or imaginal repeated exposure and are designed to help individuals confront feared objects, situations, memories, and images. It involves "remembering" or "recalling" the event or visiting the scene. The goal of exposure is to decrease the hyperarousal and negative effects that accompany traumatic reminders so the trauma thoughts are no longer paired with the overwhelming negative emotion. In addition, the intensity of intrusive reminders is reduced, which minimizes the need for avoidant behavior.

Because exposure therapy can cause some distress as children confront traumatic situations/objects, it is not often conducted in school. In addition, it requires specialized training. Use of exposure techniques in the school setting requires careful planning. Sending a child back to class after using exposure techniques too quickly can be problematic and problem behaviors affiliated with trauma triggers could occur. If a child is engaged in this therapeutic approach outside of the school setting, school staff should collaborate with the mental health professional (if parents sign a release of information) and be prepared for the discomfort and distress the child might experience. Extra support might be needed until the child has completed the therapeutic process.

Eye Movement Desensitization and Reprocessing (EMDR)

Eye Movement Desensitization and Reprocessing (EMDR) is a phased treatment approach. The goal is to diminish symptoms of PTSD by moving attention away from the feelings of fear and anxiety generated by recalling the traumatic event and using anxiety strategies to encounter and process the fear. It uses "dual stimulation" using either bilateral eye movements, tones, or taps as the client attends momentarily to past memories, present triggers, or anticipated future experiences. The therapist then helps the clients develop new associations. Research has shown it to be equally or more effective in reducing PTSD symptoms when compared with other CBT methods. There is no research of this being delivered in the school setting, but there is limited, emerging research on positive outcomes with children and adolescents. Thus, referral to a specialized, trained professional is required.

Comprehensive Services

Comprehensive services that serve both the child and their family are important for those families impacted by ongoing, traumatic stressors, particularly generational trauma. School professionals are critical team members in a system of care or wraparound services approach. School mental health professionals can be leaders in establishing these systems and ensuring long-term sustainability.

Systems of Care

Systems of care is a comprehensive service framework where school professionals and community professionals work together to provide services to the student and their family. There are six practices integral to systems of care success:

1. Student support providers in the schools work with students, their families, and all members of the school community.
2. School-based and school-focused wraparound services are used to support learning and transition.
3. School-based case managers determine needs; identify goals, resources, and activities; link children and families to other services; monitor services to ensure appropriate delivery; and advocate for change when necessary.
4. Schoolwide prevention and early intervention programs are implemented as part of a school's service delivery framework.
5. Centers are created within the school to support students and their families.
6. Family liaisons or advocates help to strengthen the role of and empower family members in their children's education and care.

While some of these practices are being implemented by schools, it has been a challenge due to under-resourced schools and community agencies. Consistent communication and collaboration between the school and the community agencies is needed, and long-term change takes patience and ongoing allocated resources. If this can occur, these type of services lead to meaningful, positive long-term changes for students and their families.

Wraparound Services

Wraparound services are not a specific therapy or a program, but a comprehensive planning process involving the child and family, community agencies, and school staff. Tailored services and supports are provided to children and their families. This approach blends multitiered positive behavior support and academic interventions to ensure success, while empowering the families to take ownership of their growth. The wraparound team includes the child and family, professional service providers (e.g., school and community mental health professionals, child's teachers and support staff, child welfare workers, law enforcement and juvenile justice personnel), and natural supports (e.g. extended family members, friends, clergy). A strengths-based assessment is conducted to help the team develop goals and identify individualized services and supports. The wraparound approach involves essential elements and values to guide the process:

1. Collective, collaborative, community-based resources and supports
2. Individualized support and strengths-based assessments
3. Culturally competent professionals and services
4. Family-centered involvement as full and active partners in every level
5. Team-driven process, involving the family, child, natural supports, agencies, and community services
6. Flexible funding and creative, adaptive approaches to resources and services

7. A balance of formal services and informal community and family resources

8. Unconditional commitment focused on resilience

9. A service/support plan developed and implemented based on an interagency, community-neighborhood collaborative process

10. Results-oriented and measurable outcomes

Outcomes show long-term positive changes for the child and family. However, a significant challenge to implementation is the extensive involvement from multiple professionals and services.

A Student's Story

Jonathan and his two older siblings have missed multiple days of school and have just been referred to the truancy officer. Before the truancy hearing, the school social worker meets with Jonathan's grandma (the primary caregiver) to conduct an interview to identify family strengths and needs. Grandma confides that she is at a loss as to how to help her grandchildren. They witnessed significant violence, followed by the death of one parent due to a drug overdose and the incarceration of their other parent. This led to their removal and placement with grandma. The family is struggling to put food on the table and oftentimes there is no money for gas. They live two blocks outside of the bussing zone, thus leaving a 1.8 mile walk for the kids. This is just too far of a walk for a seven, ten, and twelve year old, and she herself is not in good health to escort them. She sees so much potential in her grandchildren as they are respectful to her and good at their school work when they attend school, but she also knows what they have witnessed and their loss of both parents has had an impact. When this information is shared with Jonathan's counselor, the school counselor and social worker engage community supports to help the family. Jonathan confided he was too scared to tell anyone at school as he was afraid his grandma would get "in trouble."

QUESTIONS to CONSIDER

1. What supports and resources are available to help the family?

2. How could systems of care or wraparound services be helpful?

3. What school supports could be helpful?

KEY POINTS

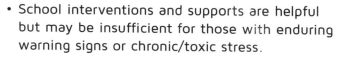

- School interventions and supports are helpful but may be insufficient for those with enduring warning signs or chronic/toxic stress.

- School and community agency partnerships can help families address generational trauma and provide parent/caregiver supports.

- Empower parents/caregivers to be partners. This can lead to systemic, positive family changes.

- School mental health professionals can be leaders in helping to establish systems of care or wraparound services.

How Can Schools Partner with Parents to Help Students Exposed to Trauma?

Trauma impacts the family system. For students with adverse childhood experiences, there is often generational and cultural trauma and caregivers whose own trauma history has often gone undiagnosed and untreated. The physiological and psychological effects of trauma begin as early as pregnancy, the maladaptive behaviors associated with trauma behaviors are often modeled for the children, and trauma interferes with quality parenting and attachment. Thus, trauma is "passed down."

Parents with trauma histories are often afraid to reach out for fear of being judged or fear that other systems may become involved (e.g. social services) that will lead to negative consequences. Others, due to their own generational trauma, may not even see it as trauma but as a normal way of life. This makes home-school communication and a trusting partnership incredibly important. School professionals may be the first ones to identify the trauma and the first ones to reach out with supports, and this may be the first time a family trusts a school professional to help.

It is also important for the school to communicate positive news to the family; if all the family hears is bad news, they will stop responding. There are going to be good days and bad days, as recovery from trauma is not a linear progression but is more like "riding waves." Some days the student (or family) may feel like they are on top of the wave, doing okay. Other days may feel like they are being engulfed by the wave. It is important for support systems to help the student (and their family) ride the waves.

Parent Education

Parents need to be educated on the signs and symptoms of stress. After exposure to an acute traumatic stressor, this could be done via dissemination of informational documents and resources and/or during a caregiver training for parents (i.e. PREPaRE Workshop 2 curriculum). This information can also be woven into parent newsletter articles or posted on a school's website.

Appendix C lists questions adapted from the ACEs study to assess for ACEs exposure in children/adolescents. The higher the number of affirmative responses, the greater the risk for developing traumatic stress responses. Parents should be encouraged to reach out for supports, particularly if there are social, emotional, behavioral, and academic difficulties. Parents (and other caregivers such as teachers and support staff) should also be encouraged to reach out for their own supports if they have multiple ACEs in their history.

A reminder: exposure alone does not mean an individual will develop traumatic stress responses. Resilient individuals, and those with supports, have protective factors that can mitigate the effects of exposure. However, affirmative responses paired with minimal to no supports and trauma reactions often indicate additional supports are needed. Parents must know how to access supports at school if their child is exhibiting the enduring warning signs listed in chapter 2.

Understanding One's Culture

Families differ in how they understand and respond to traumatic situations. Often these differences are related to one's own community or cultural norms. Understanding how one's own culture responds to traumatic situations helps to better understand how the child's friends and family members may respond. The following are questions for parents (and staff) to think about and reflect on their own cultural norms.

1. What does your community or culture view to be appropriate reactions to trauma? This allows for a better understanding of what reactions are culturally typical or within cultural norms versus what reactions indicate that additional supports may be needed.

2. How do you view or judge different types of traumatic stress reactions? Do you expect your child/student to respond like you respond? Children may respond differently than their parents due to their developmental stage, or their responses may be more like their peers. Support your child's/student's responses rather than judge them, and help your child/student understand how to process and deal with the different responses of family members and peers.

3. What type of support do you view as most helpful? This can depend on individual and family values and cultural norms. It is important to identify what supports you perceive as helpful and to be respectful of those perceived as helpful by the family (e.g., faith-based community, peers, other family members).

4. How do your own biases impact how you percieve and interpret trauma and trauma reactions. Do you have a growth mindset (belief that strengths can be cultivated)? To be a culturally competent and sensitive caregiver and educator, it is important to examine one's biases and competence in unconditionally supporting those of different races, culture, and religion.

Parents can also be encouraged to provide many supports at home (these strategies can also work for any adult in a caregiving role!). General strategies include:

1. **Listen, protect, and connect.** Careful adult attention and support is needed. Be emotionally and physically available and let your child know you are willing to pay attention and listen. Let your child's questions be the guide in talking about the traumatic event. Do not force your child to talk and do not ask detailed questions where they will feel pressure to share details they are not ready to share.

   - Protect your child by answering questions truthfully, dispelling rumors, and providing reassurance that children will be taken care of.

   - Provide reassurance that all feelings are okay. Reinforce that most reactions are normal, although it feels like life is not normal right now. Reinforce it will get easier with time, but if not, they need to ask for help.

   - Keep your child connected to familiar routines and activities. Spend extra time with your child. Encourage familiar routines and activities as they may be scared to re-engage and may need adult physical and emotional presence to do so.

2. **Teach and model activities to manage stress.** Encourage your child to listen to the body's "alarm system." Practice stress-management strategies:

   - Teach your child deep breathing techniques
   - Encourage your child to express feelings through talking, music, or art
   - Encourage your child to participate in preferred, pleasurable, and relaxing activities
   - Help reduce demands. While you do not want to completely change the expectations (remember routines help create a sense of control and

predictability), you do not want your child's to-do list to be overwhelming. Asking your child's teachers for temporary modifications can engage more choices to help foster a sense of control.

3. **Monitor your own reactions**. Be aware of your own thoughts, feelings, and behaviors. It is okay to show some emotion, but avoid losing emotional control (e.g., crying hysterically) in front of your child. Younger children, in particular, look to adults, as high levels of emotion can make the event seem even scarier. Reach out for your own supports. Taking care of yourself is an important first step, as you need to first put on your own oxygen mask in order to be able to take care of your child (a.k.a. the airline safety analogy).

4. **Take your child's perspective**. It is natural for children to worry that the event will happen again and/or worry about loved ones and friends. Think about the many ways a child's life may have changed as a result of the traumatic event (e.g., loss of a loved one; move to a new home or community; separation from supports; loss of belongings; not feeling physically or emotionally safe). Understanding their perspective helps you better understand how to help and also conveys empathy.

5. **Build resiliency**. Help your child develop coping skills.

   • Teach and model ways to regulate emotions and solve problems. Help your child understand it's okay to feel all emotions, but it's what you do with the emotions that can be helpful or harmful (e.g., it is okay to be angry and hit a pillow or release your anger through physical activity, but it is not okay to become verbally or physically aggressive toward others).

   • Teach positive and healthy ways of coping with stress, such as exercise, play, and deep breathing.

   • Help your child develop an active (or approach-oriented) coping style. Find ways to help others cope or take action to help themselves cope (e.g., community cleanup or a fundraiser).

- Promote self-confidence and self-esteem. Build on what your child already does well. If they enjoy art, have them draw a picture of how they are feeling and talk about their picture. If they enjoy writing, they can journal or write poetry about how they are feeling. For those who enjoy physical activity, encourage an outdoor activity and/or sports. If your child is social, encourage them to get together with friends and do a fun activity.

6. Reinforce the importance of existing faith and belief systems. While some may question their faith at this time, research shows these supports contribute to recovery (e.g., church group, leadership group, and activity club).

7. Encourage school connectedness and engagement. Talk to your child's teachers and work together to help your child feel more connected to school. Ensure access to positive peers and adult role models. Don't hesitate to seek professional help from a school psychologist, counselor, or social worker if needed. And don't forget, parents (and teachers) need to be connected too!

8. Promote positive self-talk. Encourage your child to think and state positive thoughts, such as "I am strong," "I'm a good kid who had a bad thing happen," "People care about me," and "It's not my fault." This helps them understand that while they may not have control over the situation, they do have control over how they respond to the situation.

9. Expect recovery. With the right supports, children can and do recover from the effects of adverse experiences. The presence of supportive relationships can be more powerful than the absence of adverse childhood experiences.

10. Don't be afraid to seek professional help. Although recovery is the rule, when trauma reactions do not begin to lessen after a week or more, consider seeking the help of a school counselor, psychologist, social worker, or school nurse. Working as a team can help us all!

Parents have a difficult job of taking care of themselves while also taking care of their children. However, they need to know they do not have to go it alone. School professionals can be a great partner in the journey of recovery.

A Parent's Story

Mr. Larson is a single dad of three elementary-aged children. He is struggling after his wife's death and has received multiple calls from the school counselor with concerns about his children's behavior in school. Two are acting out and one is withdrawing. He confided to the school counselor that he was overwhelmed. After his wife's death, he was trying to support his kids in their own grief, but he also had his own. Most days he felt like he was failing them, just going through the motions of each day and not having the emotional energy to truly be there for his kids in their anger and sadness. He knew he needed help.

QUESTIONS
to
CONSIDER

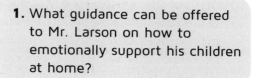

1. What guidance can be offered to Mr. Larson on how to emotionally support his children at home?

2. What supports and resources can be provided to the family?

3. What communication and collaboration needs to take place with the teachers?

4. What type of home-school communication can be established?

KEY POINTS

- Supporting the parent/primary caregiver also supports the student.
- Intervention planning must build upon family and student strengths and empower the caregiver.
- Consistent home-school collaboration is critical to an effective partnership.

Concluding Thoughts

Schools are expected to do more now than ever before. Knowledge empowers, and with that knowledge we can be part of the solution. Our students need and depend on us. Before students can focus on academics (and teachers can focus on teaching), there needs to be a positive school climate and a basic foundation of healthy attachment, self-regulation, and stress management. While schools were primarily set up to address acute trauma, we are now having to address chronic trauma. The stakes are just too high if we don't. With this newfound knowledge, we can empower, not label. We can empathize, not judge.

Below are key takeaways as we continue this important work.

1. It starts with relationships!
2. When trust is broken, it takes time to connect and trust. Be patient with each other.
3. Punishment alone does not change behavior. Teach prosocial replacement skills.
4. Teaching social-emotional skills helps students escape toxic environments and builds resiliency.
5. Keep what is best for the student(s) at the forefront of every decision.
6. One's past does not have to define whom they become in the future.
7. Focus on strengths and wellness, not on weaknesses and pathology.
8. Don't give up. We can and do make a difference!

The following quote was shared with me years ago when I was doing my student teaching (see next page). It embraces the power we have as educators and has forever remained at the forefront of my professional work.

"I've come to a frightening conclusion that I am the decisive element in the classroom.

It's my personal approach that creates the climate. It's my daily mood that makes the weather. As a teacher, I possess a tremendous power to make a child's life miserable or joyous. I can be a tool of torture or an instrument of inspiration. I can humiliate or heal. In all situations, it is my response that decides whether a crisis will be escalated or de-escalated and a child humanized or dehumanized."

—

Haim Ginott

[1] Stevens, J. (2013). Nearly 35 million children in the U.S. have experienced one or more types of childhood trauma. *ACEs Too High*. Retrieved from https://acestoohigh.com/2013/05/13/nearly-35-million-u-s-children-have-experienced-one-or-more-types-of-childhood-trauma/.

[2] "About the CDC-Kaiser ACE Study," Centers for Disease Control and Prevention, https://www.cdc.gov/violenceprevention/aces/about.html.

[3] Ibid.

[4] *Resilience: The Biology of Stress & the Science of Hope*, KPJR Films, 2016, https://kpjrfilms.co/resilience/.

[5] Dr. Nadine Burke Harris, *Resilience: The Biology of Stress & the Science of Hope*, KPJR Films, 2016, https://kpjrfilms.co/resilience/.

[6] Daniel J. Siegel and Tina Payne Bryson, *The Whole-Brain Child: 12 Revolutionary Strategies to Nurture Your Child's Developing Mind* (Bantam, 2012).

[7] Ruth A. S. Nichols, "Impact of Stress and Trauma on Emotional Development," Shared Parenting Info, July 20, 2018, https://sharedparentinginfo.com/563/.

[8, 9, 10] Brock, S. & Reeves, M. (2019). PREPaRE WS2 (3rd Ed): Mental Health Crisis Intervention: Â Responding to an Acute Traumatic Stressor in Schools. National Association of SchoolÂ Psychologists, Bethesda, MD.Â

[11] "National Disaster Recovery Framework," FEMA, https://www.fema.gov/emergency-managers/national-preparedness/frameworks/recovery.

[12] Nadine Burke Harris, *The Deepest Well: Healing the Long-Term Effects of Childhood Adversity* (New York: Houghlin Mifflin Harcourt, 2018).

[13] Eric Rossen and Katherine C. Cowan, "The Role of Schools in Supporting Traumatized Students," *Principal's Research Review*, 8(6), 1–8, 2013.

[14] Jessica Linnick, et al., "Re-examining conduct disorder through the lens of complex trauma," Conference Presentation, 2017 APA Annual Convention, Washington DC, United States.

[15] Ibid.

[16] Tony Kline, "Applying Maslow's Hierarchy of Needs in Our Classrooms," ChangeKidsLives.org, http://www.changekidslives.org/actions-4.

[17] Dr. Jack Shonkoff, *Resilience: The Biology of Stress & the Science of Hope*, KPJR Films, 2016, https://kpjrfilms.co/resilience/.

18 Center for American Progress. (2016, September 22). Counsel or criminalize: Why students of color need supports, not suspensions. Retrieved from https://cdn.americanprogress.org/wp-content/up-loads/2016/09/21142816/SupportNotSuspensions-brief.pdf.

American School Counselor Association, Educators Trust, Reach Higher (2019), School Counselors Matter https://www.schoolcounselor.org/asca/media/asca/Publications/ASCAEdTrustRHFactSheet.pdf .

19 "PREPaRE Training Curriculum," National Association of School Psychologists, https://www.nasponline.org/professional-development/pre-pare-training-curriculum.

20 *Resilience: The Biology of Stress & the Science of Hope*, KPJR Films, 2016, https://kpjrfilms.co/resilience/.

21 "SEL Impact," CASEL, https://casel.org/impact/.

22 Sandra M. Chafouleas, Austin H. Johnson, Stacy Overstreet, and Natascha M. Santos, "Toward a Blueprint for Trauma-Informed Service Delivery in Schools," *School Mental Health*, 8, 144-162, 2016, https://files.eric.ed.gov/fulltext/ED575023.pdf.

23 "PREPaRE Workshops," NASP, https://www.nasponline.org/professional-development/prepare-training-curriculum/prepare-workshops.

**ALL REFERENCES ARE AVAILABLE AS PART
OF THE DOWNLOADABLE RESOURCES.**

Acknowledgments

I would like to thank school psychology graduate students Lauren Hurley, Samantha Rudolph, and Blakely Abercrombie for their help in conducting a thorough literature review.

To my mentor and friend, Dr. Stephen E. Brock. I am forever grateful for the significant impact you have had on my life and the lives of those impacted by trauma.

Where Can I Find Out More About Trauma?

Prevention/School Climate/Crisis Intervention

www.nasponline.org
The National Association of School Psychologists (NASP) provides a multitude of resources pertaining to comprehensive school safety planning and crisis response and supports. Many resources are in handout format for downloading and/or electronic distribution.

PREPaRE School Crisis Prevention & Intervention Curriculum

- https://www.nasponline.org/professional-development/prepare-training-curriculum
- Student Psychoeducational Groups in Crisis Prevention and Intervention. School Crisis Intervention: The PREPaRE Model. (Free manual with lesson plans and worksheets to guide delivery of student psychoeducational groups for elementary to high school) https://www.csus.edu/indiv/b/brocks/Workshops/NASP/NASP%202017%20PsychoEd%20Handbook%20Revised%20April%202017.pdf

A Framework for Safe and Successful Schools (PDF document)

- https://www.nasponline.org/resources-and-publications/resources-and-podcasts/school-climate-safety-and-crisis/systems-level-prevention/a-framework-for-safe-and-successful-schools

General Crisis Resources

- https://www.nasponline.org/resources-and-publications/resources-and-podcasts/school-climate-safety-and-crisis

COVID-19 Resources

- https://www.nasponline.org/resources-and-publications/resources-and-podcasts/covid-19-resource-center

www.casel.org
The Collaborative for Academic, Social, and Emotional Learning (CASEL) provides a multitude of resources regarding the implementation of social-emotional programming to increase academic achievement and decrease behavioral and emotional challenges.

www.pbis.org
The Positive Behavioral Interventions and Supports (PBIS) website provides a multitude of free resources to support schools in the implementation of a multitiered approach to social, emotional, and behavioral supports.

Trauma Sensitive Schools

www.traumasensitiveschool.org
This website provides free, downloadable resources to help schools advocate for and implement trauma-sensitive strategies.

- *Helping Traumatized Students Learn – A Report and Policy* Agenda

- *Helping Traumatized Students Learn – Creating and Advocating for Trauma-Sensitive Schools*
- Plus, additional resources

Steps to Create a Trauma-Informed School.

- https://starr.org/wp-content/uploads/10-Steps-to-Create-a-Trauma-Informed-School-Whitepaper.pdf

  Facilitates implementation of a trauma-informed approach; includes planning and implementation activities and also checklists for ACEs

https://hearts.ucsf.edu/
Healthy Environments and Response to Trauma in Schools (HEARTS) is a whole-school, prevention and intervention approach that utilizes a multitiered system of supports (MTSS) framework to address trauma and chronic stress at the student level, staff level, and school organizational level.

Trauma Resources

https://www.nctsn.org/
The National Center for Traumatic Stress Network website provides resources to help educators better understand trauma and grief, and also provides simple and straightforward strategies educators can use to accommodate a traumatized child in the school setting.

- http://www.nctsn.org/resources/audiences/school-personnel/trauma-toolkit

Psychological First Aid

- http://www.nctsn.org/content/psychological-first-aid-schoolspfa - free download

- https://rems.ed.gov/docs/HH_Vol3Issue3.pdf - free download

ACEs

- https://www.cdc.gov/violenceprevention/acestudy/index.html

Training Tools

Trauma Informed School Video – "A San Diego Principal Takes on Trauma"

- https://www.youtube.com/watch?v=dcvQb9e-VLI

Positive School Climate Video – "Every Opportunity" - Atlanta Speech School

- https://www.youtube.com/watch?v=VxyxywShewI

Wraparound Services

Eber, L. (2008). Wraparound: A key component of school-wide systems of positive behavior supports. In E. J. Bruns & J. S. Walker (Eds.). *The resource guide to wraparound services.* Portland, OR: National Wraparound Initiative, Research and Training Center for Family Support and Children's Mental Health.

https://nwi.pdx.edu/NWI-book/Chapters/Eber-5e.3-(school-wide-support-systems).pdf

Trauma and Anxiety Management Curriculums:

- CBITS: Cognitive Behavioral Intervention for Trauma in Schools (2nd Ed)
    - https://cbitsprogram.org/
- Supports for Students Exposed to Trauma
    - https://ssetprogram.org/
- Bounce Back (K–5)
    - https://bouncebackprogram.org/
- *Worried No More: Help and Hope for Anxious Children* by Aureen Pinto Wagner.
- Coping Cat (youth), The C.A.T. Project (adolescents), and Camp Cope-A-Lot (interactive computer program) – anxiety management
    - https://www.workbookpublishing.com/

SEL Curriculums:

Kimochis: Social and Emotional Learning Curriculum

A classroom-based program that promotes social and emotional learning by teaching children the skills to understand their emotions, peacefully communicate feelings to others, develop positive relationships, manage conflicts and challenges, and make and keep friends. It also focuses on character development to be respectful, responsible, resilient, compassionate, and kind. It is highly interactive with puppet characters and feeling pillows with guidance lessons. There is also a parent curriculum for use at home.

https://www.kimochis.com/

Zones of Regulation

A systematic, cognitive behavioral approach used to teach self-regulation by categorizing feelings and states of alertness into four concrete colored zones. The Zones framework provides strategies to teach students to become more aware of and independent in controlling their emotions and impulses, manage their sensory needs, and improve their ability to problem-solve conflicts.

http://www.zonesofregulation.com

Check In Check Out (Behavior Education Program)

The Check In Check Out program (Behavior Education Program - BEP) presents students with daily/weekly goals connected to schoolwide behavior expectations. Frequent feedback and daily performance data are utilized.

Second Step (P–8)

Second Step has easy-to-teach lessons and engaging songs and games. Kids learn empathy, emotion-management, self-regulation, executive function, and problem-solving skills

https://www.secondstep.org/

Promoting Alternative Thinking Strategies—PATHS (preK–6th)

PATHS program promotes peaceful conflict resolution, emotion regulation, empathy, and responsible decision making.

http://www.pathstraining.com/main/

6 Minute SEL Lessons

6 Minute SEL Lessons is a resource to help boost core SEL skills. Contains 150 ready-made lessons and each lesson only takes six minutes. Lessons can be used as prompts during restorative circles, as warm-up activities for whole group or small groups, or as a think-pair-share activity.

https://www.lessonsforsel.com/
• website also includes free download of Racial Equity SEL cards

Psychoeducation Resources:

Julia Cook – Children's book author; many books also have activity books for psychoeducational SEL lessons

https://www.juliacookonline.com/

Books include:
Flicker of Hope
The Rules Don't Apply to Me
Soda Pop Head
Grief Is Like a Snowflake
And many more

Todd Parr – Children's book author; various SEL topics

https://www.toddparr.com/

Black Emotional and Mental Health (BEAM) – Lessons that focus on emotional wellness through accountability, self-control, emotional awareness for black, marginalized youth.

https://www.beam.community/tool-kits-education

COVID-19 – *The Adventures of Butterfly and Puppy: A Social Story About Social Distancing* by Allison Talbot. Available on Amazon.

Activity Books:

• Ann Vernon, *Thinking, Feeling, Behaving: An Emotional Education Curriculum for Children/Grades 1–6*, Revised Ed. (Research Press, 2006).

- Ann Vernon, *Thinking, Feeling, Behaving: An Emotional Education Curriculum for Children/Grades 7-12*, Revised Ed. (Research Press, 2006).
- Lisa M. Schab, *The Anxiety Workbook for Teens: Activities to Help You Deal with Anxiety and Worry* (Instant Help, 2008).
- Kate Collins-Donnelly, *Starving the Anger Gremlin: A Cognitive Behavioural Therapy Workbook on Anger Management for Young People* (Jessica Kingsley Publishers, 2012).
- R. C. Lohmann, *The Anger Workbook for Teens* (Instant Help Books, 2009)
- Lisa M. Schab, *The Self-Esteem Workbook for Teens: Activities to Help You Build Confidence and Achieve Your Goals* (Instant Help, 2013).

Professional Resources

Eric Rossen, *Supporting and Educating Traumatized Students: A Guide for School-Based Professionals, Second Edition* (New York: Oxford University Press, 2020).

Victoria B. Damani, *Crisis prevention and intervention in the classroom, Second Edition* (New York: R&L Education, 2011).

Amanda B. Nickerson, Melissa B. Reeves, Stephen E. Brock, and Shane R. Jimerson, *Identifying, Assessing, and Treating PTSD at School* (New York: Springer, 2009).

Robert B. Brooks, *The Self-Esteem Teacher: Seeds of Self-Esteem* (Treehaus Publishing, 1991).

Rosemary B. Mennuti, Ray W. Christner, Arthur Freeman, *Cognitive-Behavioral Interventions in Educational Settings: A Handbook for Practice, Second Edition* (Routledge Publishing, 2012).

Torrey A. Creed, Jarrod Reisweber, Aaron T. Beck, *Cognitive Therapy for Adolescents in School Settings* (New York: Guilford Publishing, 2011).

DOWNLOADABLE RESOURCES

The resources in this book are available for you
as a digital download!

Please visit **15minutefocusseries.com** and click this book
cover on the page. Once you've clicked the book cover,
a prompt will ask you for a code to unlock the activities.

Please enter code:

Trauma318

PREPaRE Workshop 2 (3rd Edition), Mental Health Crisis Interventions: Responding to an Acute Traumatic Stressor in Schools

This two-day workshop develops the knowledge and skills required to provide immediate mental health crisis interventions to the students, staff, and school community members who have been exposed to an acute traumatic stressor. This session also helps to build a bridge to the psychotherapeutic and trauma-informed mental health response sometimes required to address long-term challenges. This workshop is an excellent course for all school mental health professionals (and community mental health professionals who support schools) who will provide mental health crisis intervention services.

For more information regarding professional development workshops visit: https://www.nasponline.org/professional-development/prepare-training-curriculum/prepare-workshops or the book School Crisis The PREPaRE Model, Second Edition can be purchased at https://www.nasponline.org/books-and-products/products/books/titles/school-crisis-the-prepare-model-2nd-edition

Below is a summary of the specific protocols learned in the workshop. This appendix does not replace being trained in how to deliver the specific interventions but provides an important overview of the distinction between the different multi-tiered interventions.

Evaluation of Psychological Trauma	Classroom Meeting
1. **Threat Perceptions** (determined or influenced by) • Crisis event (predictability, consequences, duration, intensity) • Physical and emotional proximity • Vulnerabilities (avoidance coping, mental illness, poor emotional control, low developmental level, trauma history, "aloneness") • Adult reactions 2. **Crisis Reactions** (mental health referral indicators) • Durable (last a week or more) • Interfere with daily functioning • Acute (panic, dissociation, extreme fright) • Increased arousal (startle, hypervigilance, disturbed sleep) • Maladaptive coping (suicidal or homicidal)	1. **Introduce** the training (5 min). 2. **Provide crisis facts** (5 min). • Ensure caregivers can help children understand the crisis. 3. **Answer student questions** (5 min). • CAUTION: Don't give children unasked-for details. 4. **Refer** (as indicated) to techniques for responding to children's crisis reactions.
Caregiver Training	**Stabilization**
1. **Introduce** caregivers to the training. 2. **Provide crisis facts.** • Ensure that caregivers can help children understand the crisis. Don't give children unasked-for details. 3. **Prepare for crisis reactions.** • Normalize most reactions. • Identify pathological reactions and referral procedures. 4. **Review techniques** for responding to crisis reactions. • Identify adaptive coping techniques. • Stress importance of adult reactions. • Identify support resources.	1. Respect privacy, give physical & emotional space 2. Remain calm, quiet, and present. 3. Contact the distressed person. Ask them to listen to you. 4. Orient to person, place, & setting. 5. Describe surroundings. 6. Reestablish social support. 7. Provide reassuring crisis facts (conversation not forced). • Offer emotional assistance. • Provide practical guidance. 8. Ground the distressed person (as indicated). For young children also consider 9. Touch & place (don't force) protective arm across shoulder 10. Distract with safe questions about interests

Student Psychoeducational Group	Individual Crisis Intervention

1. **Introduce students to the lesson.**
  • Introduce facilitators. Review process and rules.
2. **Answer questions and dispel rumors.**
  • Help students understand the crisis.
  • CAUTION: Don't give unasked-for frightening details.
3. **Prepare students for crisis reactions.**
  • Normalize most reactions.
  • Identify pathological reactions and referral procedures.
4. **Empower students.**
  • Practice stress management and relaxation techniques.
  • Identify support systems.
  • Specify adaptive coping strategies.
5. **Close.**
  • Ensure that students have crisis reaction management plans.
	1. **Establish psychological contact.**
	  • Introduce self.
	  • Meet basic needs.
	  • Demonstrate empathy, respect, and warmth.
	2. **Verify readiness to proceed.**
	  • Ensure that student is emotionally stable and able to solve problems.
	3. **Identify and prioritize crisis problems.**
	  • Ask for crisis story (don't press for details).
	  • Assess lethality. Put physical and safety needs first.
	  • Identify personal and social problem-solving resources.
	4. **Address crisis problems.**
	  • Ask, facilitate, then propose solutions (empower survivors).
	  • Determine level of lethality.
	  • Determine how directive to be.
	5. **Evaluate and conclude.**
	  • Ensure movement toward crisis resolution.

Group Crisis Intervention	

1. **Introduce** the group process.
  • Identify facilitators. Review process and rules.
2. **Provide** crisis facts and dispel rumors.
  • Help students understand the crisis.
  • CAUTION: Don't give unasked-for frightening details.
3. **Share** crisis stories.
  • Ask what happened and identify common experiences.
4. **Identify** crisis reactions.
  • Ask how students feel and behave, and identify common reactions.
	5. **Empower students.**
	  • Practice stress management and relaxation techniques.
	  • Identify support systems.
	  • Specify adaptive coping strategies.
	6. **Close.**
	  • Ensure that students have crisis reaction management plans.

Questions to assess number of ACEs prevalent in their life:

1. Did a parent or other adult in the household often or very often . . .
   a) Swear at you, insult you, put you down, or humiliate you? or
   b) Act in a way that made you afraid that you might be physically hurt?

2. Did a parent or other adult in the household often or very often . . .
   a) Push, grab, slap, or throw something at you? or
   b) Ever hit you so hard that you had marks or were injured?

3. Did an adult or person at least five years older than you ever . . .
   a) Touch or fondle you or have you touch their body in a sexual way? or
   b) Attempt or actually have oral, anal, or vaginal intercourse with you?

4. Did you often or very often feel that . . .
   a) No one in your family loved you or thought you were important or special? or
   b) Your family didn't look out for each other, feel close to each other, or support each other?

5. Did you often or very often feel that . . .
   a) You didn't have enough to eat, had to wear dirty clothes, and had no one to protect you? or
   b) Your parents were too drunk or high to take care of you or take you to the doctor if you needed it?

6. Were your parents ever separated or divorced?

7. Was your mother or stepmother:
   a) Often or very often pushed, grabbed, slapped, or had something thrown at her? or
   b) Sometimes, often, or very often kicked, bitten, hit with a fist, or hit with something hard? or
   c) Ever repeatedly hit over at least a few minutes or threatened with a gun or knife?

8. Did you live with anyone who was a problem drinker or alcoholic, or who used street drugs?

9. Was a household member depressed or mentally ill, or did a household member attempt suicide?

10. Did a household member go to prison?